The Anti - Federalist Papers
(Part 1)

presented by
LENA SHIMOMURA

THE RIGHTS OF THE INDIVIDUAL VERSUS

THE POWER OF THE GOVERNMENT

Should the members of the government be elected by direct vote of the people? Should the central government of the United States be stronger than the individual state governments? Does slavery have any place in a nation dedicated to liberty? Should the government be headed by a single executive, and how powerful should that executive be? Should immigrants be allowed into the United States? Which citizens should have the vote? How should judges be appointed, and what should their role in government be? What human rights should be safe from government infringement? In 1787, these important questions and others were raised as the states debated the merits of the proposed Constitution. Along with *The Federalist Papers,* this invaluable book documents the political context in which the Constitution was born.

Contents

INTRODUCTION
The Revolutionary Background of American Constitutional Thought
Republicanism in the 1780s
Political Currents of the 1780s
The Federal Convention of 1787
The Ratification Contest
Federalist Principles
Anti-federalist Political Thought

ARRANGEMENT, USE, AND EDITING OF THE DOCUMENTS
ACKNOWLEDGMENTS
LIST OF PLANS, PROPOSALS, AND AMENDMENTS
CHRONOLOGY OF DOCUMENTS AND IMPORTANT EVENTS
SUMMARY OF OPPOSED ARGUMENTS IN FEDERALIST AND ANTI-FEDERALIST WRITINGS

PART I
THE FEDERAL CONVENTION OF 1787

James Madison to George Washington (April 16, 1787)

The Virginia Plan (May 29)
  (Edmund Randolph)

Debate on Representation (May 31)
  (Roger Sherman, Elbridge Gerry, George Mason, James Wilson, James Madison)

Debate on Executive Power (June 1)
  (Wilson, John Rutledge, Sherman, Gerry, Randolph)

Opposition to Executive Salaries (June 2)
  (Benjamin Franklin)

Opposition to a Unitary Executive (June 4)

(Mason)

Electing Representatives (June 6)
  (Gerry, Wilson, Sherman, Mason, Madison, John Dickinson)

Debate on Method of Electing Senators (June 7)
  (Sherman, Charles Pinckney, Dickinson, Wilson, George Read, Madison, Gerry)

Debate on Veto of State Laws (June 8)
  (Pinckney, Madison, Hugh Williamson, Gerry, Sherman, Wilson, Dickinson, Gunning Bedford, Pierce Butler)

The New Jersey Plan (June 15)
  (William Paterson)

Debate on the New Jersey Plan (June 16)
  (Paterson, Wilson, Randolph)

Plan for National Government (June 18)
  (Alexander Hamilton)

Opposition to the New Jersey Plan (June 19)
  (Madison)

Debate on Federalism (June 21)
  (William S. Johnson, Wilson, Madison)

Length of Term in Office for Senators (June 26)
  (Madison, Sherman, Read, Hamilton)

Debate on State Equality in the Senate (June 28-July 2)
  (Madison, Johnson, Oliver Ellsworth, Wilson, Rufus King, Hamilton, Bedford, Gouverneur Morris)

Majority Rule, the Basic Republican Principle (July 5, 13, 14)
  (Madison, Wilson)

Election and Term of Office of the National Executive (July 17, 19)
  (Morris, Sherman, Wilson, Pinckney, Mason, Madison, Gerry)

The Judiciary, the Veto, and Separation of Powers (July 21)
  (Wilson, Nathaniel Gorham, Ellsworth, Madison, Mason, Gerry, Caleb Strong, Morris, Luther Martin)

Appointment of Judges (July 21)
  (Madison, Pinckney, Randolph, Ellsworth, Morris, Gerry, Mason)

Method of Ratification (July 23)
  (Mason, Ellsworth, Madison)

Election of the Executive (July 24, 25)

(Gerry, Strong, Williamson, Ellsworth, Wilson, Madison)

First Draft of the Constitution (August 6)
(Committee on Detail; Rutledge, Chairman)

Qualifications for Suffrage (August 7, 10)
(Wilson, Morris, Ellsworth, Mason, Madison, Franklin, John F. Mercer, Rutledge, Pinckney)

Citizenship for Immigrants (August 9)
(Morris, Ellsworth, Pinckney, Mason, Madison, Butler, Franklin, Randolph, Wilson)

Executive Veto Power (August 15)
(Morris, Sherman, Wilson)

Slavery and the Constitution (August 21, 22)
(Martin, Rutledge, Ellsworth, Pinckney, Sherman, Mason, Charles C. Pinckney, Abraham Baldwin, Wilson, Gerry, Dickinson, Williamson, King, John Langdon)

Election and Powers of the President (September 4, 5, 6)
(Morris, Mason, Butler, Pinckney, Williamson, Baldwin, Wilson, Randolph, George Clymer, Hamilton)

Opposition to the Constitution (September 7, 10, 15)
(Mason, Randolph, Gerry)

Signing the Constitution (September 17)
(Franklin, Gorham, George Washington, Randolph, Morris, Williamson, Hamilton, William Blount, Gerry)

PART II
RATIFICATION OF THE CONSTITUTION

Speech of James Wilson (October 6, 1787)

THE NEED FOR ENERGY IN GOVERNMENT (Explained in Federalist Numbers 1-8, 15-32, 34-36, 73-77)

"John DeWitt," Essays I and II (October 22 and 27, 1787)

Speeches of Patrick Henry (June 5 and 7, 1788)

Amendments Proposed by the Anti-federalists (February 7 and June 27, 1788)

Amendments to the Constitution (June 27, 1788)

Amendments Proposed by the Rhode Island Convention (March 6, 1790)

PREVENTING TYRANNY UNDER THE NEW CONSTITUTION (Explained in Federalist Numbers 9-14, 33, 37-51, 78-85)

"Centinel," Number I (October 5, 1787)

Address of the Pennsylvania Minority (December 18, 1787)

Letters from the Federal Farmer, I and II (October 8 and 9, 1787)

"Brutus," Essays I, VI, X-XII, and XV (October 18 and December 27, 1787; January 24 and 31, February 7, and March 20, 1788)

THE MEANING OF GOVERNMENT BY CONSENT (Explained in Federalist Numbers 57-72)

"John DeWitt," Essay III (November 5, 1787)

"Cato," Letters V and VII (November 22, 1787; January 3, 1788)

"Brutus," Essays IV and XVI (November 29, 1787; April 10, 1788)

Speeches of Melancton Smith (June 20-27, 1788)

APPENDIX I: The Articles of Confederation 1777 (1781)

APPENDIX II: The Constitution of the United States of America

APPENDIX III: Principal Speakers at the Federal Convention of 1787

ANNOTATED BIBLIOGRAPHY

INDEX OF IDEAS

Introduction

*The Revolutionary Background
of American Constitutional Thought*

For anyone interested in political thought in action, the United States during the 1770s and 1780s is perhaps the most exciting period in the country's history. The discussion of political ideas that accompanied the American Revolution was seminal to the effort in 1787-1788 to draft and ratify a new constitution for the United States. In the years before 1776, as tension increased between Great Britain and her North American dominions, the rapidly maturing colonies were a laboratory of proposals and revised forms of union and confederated government. Each colony was more or less self-governing under its own "constitution," but officials on both sides of the Atlantic probed for a more satisfactory relationship between the colonies and the mother country. The eleven years between the Stamp Act Crisis (1765) and the Declaration of Independence (1776) were years of vigorous, creative political thinking which produced hundreds of pamphlets, newspaper articles, and other writings on questions of representative government and confederation. Writers in Great Britain, too, debated basic political principles and regarded the many proposals for governing the empire as part of the quest for freer, eventually more democratic government.

Political independence, moreover, required new modes of thinking not only about the government but also about national identity. Initially, Britons in America often felt a sharp sense of loss in their repudiation of loyalty to the mother country. Gone or discredited were important parts of the body politic and their undergirding ideas. Revolutionists challenged the House of Lords, military institutions and traditions, and even the monarch himself—symbol and embodiment of the nation. Colonials who still thought of England as "home" regretted, too, the distancing from a cherished land and culture; Salisbury Plain and London, Shakespeare and Milton, the ale house and the parish church remained deep in the consciousness—or subconsciousness—of many transatlantic Britons. Americans were uneasy about giving up this national identity and hence moved slowly and reluctantly toward independence. Many remained "loyalists" because they could not countenance such traumatic loss. Yet, by 1776, the "radical change in the principles, opinions, sentiments, and affections [that] was the real American Revolution," as John Adams put it, had taken place: Americans no longer thought of themselves as members of the British body politic; they were no longer part of what they, and most enlightened European opinion, often regarded as the freest, best-governed nation in the world.

New institutions and new ideas of government were needed, then, to replace the rejected British models. Yet, as the revolutionary tracts showed, and as the debate over the new constitution would demonstrate anew, Americans had very little beyond British ideology and experience with which to fashion a new nationhood. All the best-known writers—Harrington, Locke, Hutcheson, Algernon Sidney, Swift, Trenchard and Gordon, Price, Burgh, and even the works of Voltaire and Montesquieu idealizing British government—focused American attention on English history and thought. Within this thoroughly British pattern, however, American political thinkers began to express vital differences in emphasis. Traditional, Tory ideas had much less weight in America than they had in Britain. Ancient institutions such as the Church, the nobility, and the common law weakened in the New World. The palaces and fortresses of authority could not cross the Atlantic Ocean. On the other hand, "radical Whig" thought, emphasizing openness and freedom, loomed proportionately larger in America. A century and one half of physical separation and relatively isolated development had nurtured what in many ways were distinctive societies. As political leaders sought after 1776 to move from colony to country, they used British concepts and precedents, but they also fashioned anew for a new nation in a New World. To an initial revolution in loyalty which repudiated a nationality, Americans had to add a second revolution in purpose that would form ideas and institutions for a new polity.

Between 1776 and 1787, then, Americans undertook to create a new republic. They had to articulate and establish, perhaps beginning with revised understandings of human nature itself, basic principles and institutions of free government. Following the lead of Tom Paine in *Common Sense* (1776), many dreamed that the overthrow of oppressive, irrational customs and authority might be followed by a paradisiacal age when only the mildest and simplest bonds of self-government would be necessary. A western Massachusetts town resolved in 1776 that "what is the fundamental Constitution of this province, what are the undeniable Rights of the people, the powers of the Rulers, how often to be elected by the people, etc." were matters to be determined explicitly and anew by the people. Though John Adams believed Paine's ideas a "Star of Disaster," and warned that it was "safest to proceed in all established modes to which the people have been familiarized by habit," he still saw in Independence "Rays of Ravishing Light and Glory." Americans would create, as they announced on their great seal, *novus ordo seclorum*, "a new order of the ages." The new government to be fashioned in the United States might become a model for the world.

Beginning with New Hampshire in January 1776, every state drafted at least one constitution before 1787 (Connecticut and Rhode Island, without royal governors before 1776, merely had to remove references to Great Britain from colonial charters). Thus the new states added to the theoretical debates of the Revolutionary era a considerable practical experience in drafting and inaugurating new, constitutional governments. They tried many often novel proposals for legislative, executive, and judicial departments. By 1787, in a famous calculation by Thomas Jefferson, the new states had had eleven times thirteen, or nearly 150, years of experience in republican government. On the whole Jefferson thought the experiments remarkably successful, proving that the people were capable of governing themselves.

Mindful of the oppressions of their last British governors, most states established legislative supremacy based on the principle of consent in their new constitutions. Pennsylvania gave broad powers to an annually-elected single-house (unicameral) legislature. In Virginia and other states, the legislature elected the governor and often had the power to appoint judges and other officials. In some states, though, notably New York and Massachusetts, the executive had more power and was elected directly by the qualified voters. Maryland chose the upper house by means of an elector college similar to that eventually put into the federal constitution. Bills of rights were drafted and debated in every state. Writing and ratifying the Articles of Confederation led to further discussion of principles and forms of government. By 1787, not only had the theory of self-government been widely debated, but virtually every conceivable device for implementing it had been suggested, if not tried.

As had been true during the long debate over "representation" within the British Empire before 1776, much attention focused on giving voice to the undistorted and uncorrupted will of the people. Small districts, annual elections, rotation in office, versions of referendum and recall, and unicameral legislatures were among the devices tried to tic representatives to that will. Intense rivalries, clash of interests, and manipulation of voters and representatives, though, seemed often to lead legislative governments into biased and unwise measures. Many states with two-house (bicameral) legislatures, and some with frankly aristocratic upper houses, even found that prolonged deliberation and checks on popular will could result in more dispassionate and practical legislation. By 1787 Americans had tried many devices of representative government, and had discussed at length the more sophisticated dilemmas it posed.

The liabilities of executive weakness had by 1787 also become apparent. Jefferson and Madison considered the impotent governorship of Virginia "the worst part of a bad constitution." The governor, elected by the legislature and required to act only with the consent of a council also elected by the legislature, was simply unable to govern. The elections of the governor and council became occasions for intrigue and influence-swapping of the worst sort. As experience with elective rather than hereditary or appointed executives accumulated, furthermore, a new and intriguing possibility emerged: the elective governor might himself become a legitimate part of government by consent when he vetoed laws, made appointments, or commanded the militia. Thus election of the governor by the people was a potentially effective *extension* of popular influence, rather than a checking of it as had normally been the case under a monarchical executive. As James Wilson would put it in 1790, with executives elected by the people and thus drawn from the same source as legislatures, "they who execute and they who administer the laws, are as much the servants, and therefore as much the friends of the people, as those who make them."

The judiciary also came under reconsideration. Experiments with legislative appointment of judges, or even election by the people, undertaken on democratic principles, seemed often to subject judges to political pressures that hindered impartiality and "equal justice." A few years' experience in Virginia with legislature-appointed judges had led, in Madison's opinion, to the sacrifice of "private rights" and the exposure of judges to "all the corruptions of the two other departments." Instead, foreshadowing provisions for the new federal judiciary, Madison favored executive appointment, fixed salaries, and life tenure to shield judges from legislative intrigue and popular sentiment.

In another effort to resist, as Madison put it, "the maxim…that the interest of the majority is the political standard of right and wrong," many leaders sought to establish written constitutions, with their bills of rights, clear definitions of procedure, and careful limitations of power, as fundamental law, above legislative or executive authority. Massachusetts and other states elected special conventions to draft constitutions and then held special elections to ratify them to underscore the supremacy and the republican character of constitutional provisions. These solemn, deliberate acts of the people established a "higher law" that a majority of the legislature or even of the people would be forbidden to violate.

American political thought and experience after 1776 in fact highlighted a tension built into the Declaration of Independence which proclaimed in one clause that certain rights were "unalienable," and in another that "Governments...derive their just powers from the consent of the governed." Rights to life, liberty, and the pursuit of happiness were not to be submitted to a vote or to depend on the outcome of elections; that is, not even the consent of the governed could legitimately abridge them. But it was nonetheless possible that the people, through their elected representatives, might sanction laws violating "unalienable" rights. Suppose legislatures, state or national, passed laws abridging freedom of the press, or violating liberty of conscience, or permitting default on contracts, as happened in the 1780s. Which principle had priority, that of "consent" or that of "unalienable rights"? Unless it could be assured that all, or at least a majority, of the people would always protect "unalienable rights," which few thought likely, the American Revolutionists seemed committed to propositions not always compatible. The Federal Constitution of 1787 was one effort to contain the tension, and the debate over its ratification often revolved around whether the framers had properly adjusted the balance of the two principles. Virtually all the members of the Federal Convention, and both sides in the ratification struggle, sought to fulfill the purposes of the Declaration of Independence to both protect rights and insure government by consent. The key differences arose over which purpose to emphasize and what mechanisms of government best assured some fulfillment of each. The separation from Great Britain and eleven years of independent state and national government had left Americans with an uncertain national identity, an intriguing republican idealism, and an intricate array of unresolved tensions and practical problems.

Republicanism in the 1780s

As the Federal Convention assembled in May 1787 its members did agree, though, on some basic principles and use of terms. All believed in government by consent, which in eighteenth-century understanding included (1) constitutional monarchy, where the monarch's powers were limited and where the government included an assembly elected by the people; (2) a republic, meaning some form of representative government without a hereditary executive; and (3) democracy, which meant either town-meeting style democracy or simply the direct voice of the people within a government. The Revolutionary struggle against the government of George III left even constitutional monarchy in ill-repute in America. (Many leaders, however, including at times John Adams and Alexander Hamilton, continued to think it theoretically the form most likely to insure freedom and good government.)

Equally discredited was "mere democracy" which still meant, as Aristotle had taught, rule by the passionate, ignorant, demagogue-dominated "voice of the people." This was sure to produce first injustice, then anarchy, and finally tyranny. Hence, virtually all shades of opinion reviled monarchy and democracy, and, publicly at least, affirmed republicanism. (This republicanism of the 1780s was not in principle different from what in Britain and America by mid-nineteenth century was generally called representative democracy. The founders would not have been opposed to the modern connotations of the word "democracy," nor would they have used the word "republic" to mark out a distinction from those connotations. In scorning "democracy," eighteenth-century theorists had in mind Aristotle's picture of a heedless, emotional, manipulated populace that would still be denigrated by most modern democratic theorists.)

By 1787, republicanism, then, was positioned between monarchy and "mere democracy." As it benefited from the experience of the years after 1776 and struggled to contain the tension between "unalienable rights" and majority rule, republicanism became both more moderate and more intricate. A broadly based lower house of a legislature continued to be basic to government by consent, but, increasingly, the election of other officials came to be regarded as good republican practice. Also, mindful of colonial experience and following the arguments of Montesquieu, the idea that the legislative, executive, and judicial powers had to be "separated," made to "check and balance" each other in order to prevent tyranny, gained wide acceptance. This often validated devices of government that would restrain or "refine" the will of the majority in order to protect rights, or "higher law."

Thus, while eighteenth-century American republicanism was committed to the sovereignty of the people, it was also a complicated approach to government. It opposed traditional, monarchical tyranny, but was equally hostile to mob rule. It also sought balancing and refining devices that would at once restrain the power of rulers, encourage the better judgment of the people, and enable the union to defend itself in a dangerous world. Edmund Burke stated the problem succinctly: "to make a government requires no great prudence; settle the seat of power, teach obedience, and the work is done. To give freedom is still more easy. It is not necessary to guide; it only requires to let go the rein. But to form a free government, that is, to temper together the opposite elements of liberty and restraint in one conscious work, requires much thought; deep reflection; a sagacious, powerful, and combining mind." Madison's formulation in Federalist No. 51 made the same point: "You must first enable the government to control the governed; and in the next place, oblige it to control itself"—as much a need in a republic as in any other form of government.

In a way, to oblige government to "control itself" was more difficult in the new United States than it was in Europe. There, "balance of power" theorists made use of the essentially different orders of traditional society—king, lords, commons, or first, second, and third estates—to achieve equilibrium in government. Thus British government preserved balanced freedom by giving each of the distinct—separately derived—orders of society a means of self-defense. The monarch, the House of Lords, and the House of Commons each had effective legislative voice. The balance was enduring because the king and the nobility and the commoners were formally and permanently separate. But in the United States, without a hereditary monarch or nobility, and without politically powerful bishops or other privileged elements formally distinct from "the people," how could checks and balances work? What real balance could there be when ultimately, as republican theory required, all legitimate power came from one entity, the people? Could the separation of powers among levels and branches of governments all resting on consent provide checks like those arising from the distinct orders of a hierarchical society? Were, then, the ideas of deriving all just power from the consent of the governed, and genuine balance of powers, mutually exclusive? Yet another complicated problem faced the framers and ratifiers of 1787-1788.

The response, drawn in part from the ideas of David Hume but best elaborated by James Madison, was to try to build into the mechanism of government itself enough variations on election, powers, term of office, and complication of function to *create* separate interests and perspectives. Thus, for example, even though an upper and a lower house of the legislature might each *eventually* derive from the people, different districts, different terms of office, different modes of election, and different definitions of authority would create balances of power. Complex arrangements for appointing and giving power to other officials, and "refinements" of popular will through devices like an electoral college, it was theorized, would become further effective substitutes for the balances inherent in the lasting divisions within traditional societies. Could mere complication of government, together with devices to "refine" the expression of majority will, without departing fundamentally from the principle of consent, protect basic rights both from potential tyrants within government and from popular passions? The intention was to temper idealism with realism, and to substitute complexity for balance of orders. The challenge offered wide scope for political theorists as well as practical strategists as the time approached to revise the Federal Constitution.

Political Currents of the 1780s

These difficult and important theoretical problems existed at the Federal Convention amid a welter of clashing interests, social distinctions, ethnic diversities, religious backgrounds, and disparities of wealth. Differences over geography, commerce, religion, customs, land speculation, slavery, and credit influenced proposals for structures of government and sometimes required compromise of principle as well as of interests. These concerns, especially that of the New England states to regulate commerce by majority vote in Congress, and of Georgia and South Carolina to keep open the slave trade (settled by compromise; see pp. 153-58), had an impact on many decisions. The Constitution also gave implicit sanction to private property (including slaves) and otherwise sustained the planter-yeoman/farmer/mercantile society that had emerged in the thirteen newly independent states. Yet, the Constitution as drafted also reflects the ebb and flow of debate over principles of government. In fact, there are some signs that the various special interests represented at the Convention counteracted and often nullified each other and thus in a way gave scope to discussion of basic constitutional issues. There is little evidence, in any case, that determined factions—creditors, land speculators, merchants, slave owners, or any others—implanted in the draft constitution a self-interested mode of government inconsistent with republican principles.

The principle of consent, furthermore, since it was thought of largely as applying to those with a material stake in society (land, securities, slaves, mercantile property, tax payments, etc.), was less inclusive in the eighteenth century than it would become two hundred years later. Property qualifications for voting and officeholding were common, and women were barred from doing either. Most extreme, black slaves were not regarded as part of the political community and hence were entirely denied participation and protection of rights. Though some advanced thinkers saw the inconsistencies in these limitations (especially of slave owners and slave traders proclaiming the blessings of liberty) and cried out against them, sentiment in 1787 had not generally reached the point where universal suffrage would be on the agenda of constitution framers. Thus the Convention ignored those issues by accepting the guidelines already existing in state constitutions and in the Articles of Confederation. Though this did not advance the causes of enlarged suffrage and abolition of slavery, at the same time, deliberately, there were no explicit barriers in the Constitution to liberalization when sentiment within any state moved in that direction. States were able to abolish slavery, and voting for members of the lower house in Congress was to carry the same limitations—or lack of limitation

—as for the lower house of the state legislature. The Convention had to find mechanisms of government that would guarantee the power of the people to decide economic as well as other matters, and protect the "unalienable rights" gained by the Revolution.

These theoretical and practical concerns persisted as the new nation struggled to survive, first in war and then in peace. As the states drafted and revised their constitutions, they also worked to form a confederal constitution. The *ad hoc* actions of the Continental Congresses, setting aside British authority and fighting the Revolutionary War, had to be formalized and a permanent form of government established. Congress approved "Articles of Confederation" in 1777 that were finally ratified (by all the states) and became the basis for national government in 1781. They were the first American constitution. Almost at once, though, complaints arose about their weakness and inefficiency. "Nationalists" such as Robert Morris, Alexander Hamilton, James Madison, James Wilson, and George Washington agreed that the Articles were inadequate and made various proposals for strengthening them. They sought especially to give Congress wider taxing power, more control over interstate and foreign commerce, and power to compel state compliance with acts of Congress. Since the Articles required unanimous consent of the states for amendment, proposals for change were easily blocked. A conference at Mount Vernon in 1785, though, which settled navigation, boundary, and other disputes between Maryland and Virginia, encouraged the idea of a larger meeting to cope with problems apparently stymied in Congress under the Articles. A convention at Annapolis in September 1786, asking all the states to discuss interstate commerce regulation, failed because most states did not send delegates. It did, however, call for another convention to meet in May 1787 in Philadelphia. A heightened sense of futility in Congress and disarray in the nation (Shays' rebellion flared that winter) led Congress and all states except Rhode Island to endorse that call. Hence, the fifty-five delegates who came to the Federal Convention of 1787 (others appointed did not come at all) had in mind generally to strengthen the Articles, but beyond that there was little agreement on how extensively and in what way to do that.

The Federal Convention of 1787

The debates of the Convention, known to us largely through notes taken by James Madison during its deliberations, flowed through readily discernible stages. The largely favorable reception by the Convention of the "Virginia Plan" (see pp. 7-12), conceived by Madison and agreed to by the Virginia delegation, implied that the Convention intended to frame a new government rather than merely amend the Articles of Confederation, as most delegates had been instructed to do. For two weeks the delegates debated representation, executive powers, state-national relations, and other basic matters. Though the Convention voted down the clause in the Virginia Plan giving Congress the power to "negative" "improper" state laws, in general there was surprising support for provisions to strengthen the national government. On June 13 the Convention accepted nineteen resolves largely following the Virginia Plan. The "small state" forces, however, still opposed bitterly the tentative switch from an equal vote for each state in the national legislature (as under the Articles of Confederation) to representation according to the population.

The Convention entered a new phase on June 15 when William Paterson introduced what became known as the "New Jersey Plan" (see pp. 39-48), retaining the equality of the states and other provisions closer to the Articles. The challenge had been made, and for a month the delegates debated state equality with increased passion and rancor, sought compromises, and struggled to prevent disruption of the Convention. Madison, James Wilson, Rufus King, and other proponents of proportional representation stood firm. Paterson, Luther Martin of Maryland, and other small-state delegates insisted just as strongly on state equality, while the Convention conciliators, mainly Benjamin Franklin and William Samuel Johnson of Connecticut, suggested compromise. A grand committee, appointed to settle the deadlocked issue, reported on July 5 recommending the so-called "Great Compromise." The lower house would have representation according to population, and the states would be equal in the upper house. Though Madison and Wilson opposed the compromise because to them it violated the vital republican principle of majority rule, most of the delegates were ready to accept an accommodation. On July 16, the Convention approved the "Great Compromise."

Having settled this major point, the Convention considered, in ten days of important debate, the powers and election of the executive, the judiciary, the method of ratification, and the powers of Congress. After making some tentative decisions and deferring others, on July 26 the Convention appointed a committee of detail to arrange and systemize what had been done so far and to make proposals on unsettled matters. Its report (see pp. 122-134), made on August 6, was the first document before the Convention to resemble the final constitution. Perhaps most notable, instead of the broad power in the Virginia Plan for Congress "to legislate in all cases to which the separate States are incompetent," the draft enumerated the powers of Congress. Madison and other advocates of broad national power came to favor a more careful definition of congressional power after the adoption of what they regarded as the flawed "Great Compromise." They were unwilling to so generally empower a body where a few states containing a small minority of the population could have a deciding voice. Small-state delegates, on the other hand, assured of an equal voice in the Senate, became increasingly willing to put power in the hands of the central government, a circumstance that led in time to the quick ratification of the Constitution by most of the small states.

For more than a month, August 7-September 10, the Convention debated, clause-by-clause, the articles of the draft constitution. As the delegates thus settled matters of detail and accepted the practical compromise between New England and the deep South states on slavery and commercial regulation (see pp. 153-58), they continued to dispute the powers of the executive department and its relation to the Senate. How to elect the executive, how he might exercise his veto, and how he might be joined with the Senate in appointive and treaty-making powers, continued to vex and divide the delegates. By September 10, after several referrals of unsettled matters to select committees, the Convention felt it had sufficiently resolved all questions to entrust its work to a committee on arrangement and style. The actual draft of the final document seems to have been executed by Gouverneur Morris.

As the Constitution took final shape, however, it was apparent that three delegates still at the Convention, Edmund Randolph and George Mason of Virginia and Elbridge Gerry of Massachusetts, did not approve it. Before and after the committee on arrangement and style did its work, they complained about many particulars, but mainly opposed the scope of powers given to the new federal government. (Their objections, reprinted on pp. 166-71, in fact anticipated many of the arguments anti-federalists would offer in the ratification debates.) Nonetheless thirty-nine delegates approved their work, and after a few changes in detail, moved, with the unanimous consent of all states present, to submit the constitution to the Confederation Congress and to the people of the states.

The Ratification Contest

The ratification struggle began with a clever move by the proponents of the new constitution: since sentiment in the country was hostile to the idea of a national government and preferred a confederation, or federation (the words were synonymous in the eighteenth century), the proponents called themselves "federalists" even though the new document was not, strictly speaking, a federation, a league of governments, as the old Articles were. In fact, the new constitution, as Madison explained carefully in Federalist No. 39, was a "composite," partly national in that some powers impinged directly on the people (most notably the taxing power and the election of the House of Representatives) and partly federal in that the states acted as "units" of the central government (most notably in the election of the Senate). By taking the popular word "federal" to denote the new constitution, its backers gained an important "image" victory for themselves. The word "federal" came eventually to mean the form of government embodied in the new Constitution, just as "confederation" came to mean the more strictly "league of states" idea of the Articles of Confederation and eventually the "Confederacy" of 1861-1865. The foes of ratification, moreover, were left with the negative designation, "anti-federalists." (The term "federalist" here, uncapitalized, refers to the proponents of the new constitution, 1787-1789, and is a different group from the political party formed in the 1790s, called "Federalist," usually capitalized.)

Important backers of the new constitution, most notably Alexander Hamilton and James Madison, returned to New York (where the Articles of Confederation Congress was in session) to organize their campaign for ratification. With Hamilton taking the initiative, he, Madison, and John Jay agreed to write a series of essays for New York newspapers explaining and defending the new Constitution. They used the pseudonym "Publius," the legendary law-giver of the Roman republic extolled by Plutarch, in addressing "the People of the State of New York." Jay's illness during the winter of 1787-1788 limited his contribution to only five of the eighty-five essays. Hamilton wrote fifty-one and Madison twenty-nine (the long dispute over authorship of some essays is now settled; Madison wrote all the essays he designated as his in old age). Anxious to get the systematic argument for the new Constitution before the public, Hamilton and Madison hurried three or four essays a week to the newspapers between October 27, 1787, and April 2, 1788. In general, Hamilton wrote the essays on the need for a more energetic government, on the powers of Congress, and on the executive and judicial departments, while Madison explained the nature of the federal system, the formal and informal checks and balances, and the House of Representatives and the Senate. At the time, however, readers did not know who "Publius" was, and saw the *Federalist* as a comprehensive, single-minded advocacy of the Constitution. At the same time other federalist essays and speeches appeared in the newspapers, and the major anti-federalist series of essays, "Centinel," "Cato," "Brutus," and "The Federal Farmer," came out initially in Philadelphia and New York newspapers, and were soon reprinted throughout the country.

As the theoretical arguments developed before the public, separate ratification struggles took place in each state. Reflecting satisfaction over the state equality in the Senate, and anxious for protection within a stronger union, conventions in three small states, Delaware, New Jersey, and Georgia, ratified early and unanimously. Connecticut was also strongly federalist and ratified readily (128-40), while the vagaries of Pennsylvania politics, plus the zeal of James Wilson and other federalists, produced an early federalist victory (46-23) there, too. Thus, when the closely divided Massachusetts convention met in January 1788, five states had already ratified. After a long, spirited debate, and some clever maneuvering by the federalists, the Massachusetts convention voted on February 16, 1787, 187-168, to ratify.

This close vote, and the strength of the anti-federalists in the critical states of Virginia and New York, created an air of uncertainty during the first six months of 1788. The eventual, easy ratifications by Maryland (63-11) and South Carolina (149-73) in April and May cheered the federalists; only one more state would need to ratify to implement the new government. Yet, awareness that anti-federalists were dominant in New Hampshire, that Rhode Island and North Carolina were hostile, and that the vital states of Virginia and New York might not ratify, left the issue in balance as the Virginia convention assembled in June. There, in the most important of the ratification contests, Madison, Randolph, and other federalists achieved a debating victory over George Mason, Patrick Henry, and their anti-federal allies. Virginia voted to ratify, 89-79, on June 25, and in the meantime New Hampshire had enough shifted its position to ratify, 57-47, on June 21. With ten states having ratified, establishment of the new government was certain. Faced with this circumstance, the New York convention, though its delegates were elected largely as anti-federalists (46-19), nonetheless after thorough debate voted to ratify, 30-27. The North Carolina convention voted against ratification, 193-75, while Rhode Island refused even to call a convention. North Carolina ratified the constitution and joined the union in November 1789, and Rhode Island did so in May 1790.

Federalist Principles

As this political struggle progressed, crucial theoretical differences clarified. The federalists on the whole saw and sought the benefits more effective, energetic government could bring even, perhaps especially, in a republic (see Federalist Nos. 1, 23). Well aware of the tendency of confederations and small, vulnerable republics to be merely provincial, to quarrel among themselves, and to be gobbled up by more united, powerful nations (see Nos. 18-20), the federalists sought the stability and strength that could come from union and from steady, effective government. As James Wilson saw with particular clarity, strong government could as much serve the people when controlled by them as it could injure them when it was hostile to them. Therefore, the need to limit the powers of government so important during the long struggle to end the tyranny of kings was perhaps misguided when the government was not alien or from above, but *of the people* (see No. 70). The goal, then, was not simply the *limitation* of the powers of the executive, or even of the government as a whole, but the insurance of its faithfulness to the people and of the stability and wisdom of its enactments. To Hamilton, Madison, and other federalists, government in the United States, even though more fully republican than any other in the world, had also often been weak, unstable, and foolish. Foreign intrigue, domestic insurrection, bankruptcy, and dismemberment all threatened the new nation, and, in the opinion of the federalists, could only be avoided by a stronger union (see Nos. 2-8).

Despite this sharp critique, the federalists still thought of themselves as heirs to the American Revolution and sincere friends of government by consent. To them the ideals of human rights and rule by the people required not suspicion of government but *use* of it. They were confident that human ingenuity could devise mechanisms that would at once protect liberty, allow effective government, and rest on the consent of the people (see Nos. 10, 37). It was possible both to give sufficient powers to the House of Representatives and to the president, and to guard against the abuse of those powers. It was only prudent to erect barriers against tendencies toward greed, passion, and selfish ambition in any human government, but it was also important to benefit from wise and good rule (see Nos. 51, 78). If good government was impossible when "the people" chose their own rulers, then the very idea of government by consent stood condemned (see No. 57). The federalists believed the new Constitution provided effective resolution of these intricacies.

They also had high hopes that with the stability and energy of the new Constitution the nation might expand and progress rapidly. The federalists sought agricultural and commercial growth that would bring wealth and prosperity to all the people, and they saw the national government as a guide and partner in the westward expansion of the nation (see No. 14). They also supposed that the nation needed vigor and power in order to survive and exert its influence in the dangerous but opportunity-laden international scene. In short, the federalists sought English-style commercial growth, domestic prosperity, and world power, which they thought were compatible with Revolutionary ideals of freedom and self-government. They believed the new Constitution furnished the means for achieving those goals.

Anti-federalist Political Thought

Perceiving these aspirations and purposes, the anti-federalists were at once skeptical and disheartened. They saw in federalist hopes for commercial growth and international prestige only the lust of ambitious men for a "splendid empire" where, in the time-honored way, the people would be burdened with taxes, conscription, and campaigns (see Patrick Henry and "John DeWitt"). Uncertain that any government over so vast a domain as the United States could be controlled by the people, the anti-federalists saw in the enlarged powers of the central government only the familiar threats to the rights and liberties of the people. The federal judiciary, for example, seemed like simply another magistry removed from the people that would enforce harsh and arbitrary laws (see "Brutus," Nos. 11, 12, 15). The broad power to lay and collect taxes, the president's role as commander-in-chief, Congress' authority to pass any laws "necessary and proper" to carry out its enumerated powers, and the "supreme law" and treaty-making powers, all seemed unbounded and at least potentially tyrannical. A persistent thrust in anti-federal thought, then, was both to withdraw some of the explicit powers given to the national government and to restrain with further checks and balances the exercise of its remaining powers. The anti-federalists were, in a sense, "men of little faith" as both contemporary and modern critics have charged, but this was true only within their fear that centralized power tended to become arbitrary and impersonal. The anti-federalists came to these views more readily, of course, because the Whig rhetoric of eighteenth-century British radicalism and the ideology of the American Revolution were filled with suspicions of power, especially distant, centralized power. These arguments were now handy for use against other advocates of such power.

The anti-federalists also had a positive idealism of their own, a republican vision they thought far closer to the purpose of the American Revolution than the political and commercial ambitions of the federalists. The anti-federalists looked to the Classical idealization of the small, pastoral republic where virtuous, self-reliant citizens managed their own affairs and shunned the power and glory of empire. To them, the victory in the American Revolution meant not so much the big chance to become a wealthy world power, but rather the opportunity to achieve a genuinely republican polity, far from the greed, lust for power, and tyranny that had generally characterized human society. Was it possible, they asked themselves, to found society on other bases and with other aspirations that would nourish the virtue and happiness of all the people? Could they break the self-fulfilling cycle where selfish people needed to be controlled by checks and balances which in turn required and encouraged more and more self-seeking by the people?

To the anti-federalists this meant retaining as much as possible the vitality of local government where rulers and ruled could see, know, and understand each other. Thus they cherished the Revolutionary emphasis on state and local councils and committees, and the Articles of Confederation where the central government rested entirely on the states. The idea of self-government was tied inextricably to something like a town meeting directness or at least to a state legislature of many annually elected representatives who would really know the people of their districts. Each "district," furthermore, would be a town or ward or region conscious of its own particular identity rather than being some amorphous, arbitrary geographic entity (see "John DeWitt"). Only with such intimacy could the trust, goodwill, and deliberation essential to wise and virtuous public life be a reality. Anything else, even though resting in some fashion on the consent of the people, would not really be self-government.

The intense anti-federalist suspicions of corruption, greed, and lust for power were directed generally at those who ruled from on high and without restraint. Corruption and tyranny would be rampant as they always had been when those who exercised power felt little connection with the people. This would be true, moreover, for elected representatives, as well as for kings and nobles and bishops, who lived in a distant capital milieu where power, intrigue, and wealth exerted their baneful influence. The more remote and distantly powerful a government was, the more visions of imperial Rome or Versailles or London came to mind with all their venality, cynicism, corruption, and neglect of the people (see "Cato"). Would some future capital of the United States be as filled with courtiers, courtesans, military heroes, and superfluous officeholders as London or Paris or St. Petersburg? The anti-federalists thought so under a constitution that consolidated power in a central government remote from the people.

On the other hand, legends of the Greek and Roman republics, the maturing ideology of natural rights, and the substantial experience of local self-government in the New World seemed to offer a far more alluring prospect. *If* the basic decency in human nature, most evident among ordinary people at the local level amid family, church, school, and other nourishing institutions, could impinge directly and continuously on government, then perhaps it too might be kept virtuous and worthy of confidence. Then, instead of endless suspicion of and guarding against the evil and corruption of government, it might be possible to trust it and use it for the public benefit. The result might even be a society where honest, hardworking people could enjoy the fruits of their labor, where institutions encouraged and rested on virtue rather than greed, where officials were servants of the people rather than oppressors, and where peace and prosperity came from vigilant self-confidence rather than from conquest and dominion (see Patrick Henry). Anti-federalists saw mild, grassroots, small-scale governments in sharp contrast to the splendid edifice and overweening ambition implicit in the new Constitution—and, indeed, heralded by Publius and its other proponents. The first left citizens free to live their own lives and to cultivate the virtue (private and public) vital to republicanism, while the second soon entailed taxes and drafts and offices and wars damaging to human dignity and thus fatal to self-government.

The anti-federalist ideal emerged most clearly and practically in its understanding of what representation and government by consent could really mean. Instead of seeking to insulate officials from popular influence, as, for example, Publius argued federal judges should be (Federalist No. 78), anti-federalists sought to insure the public good by requiring close association. If legislators, for example, rather than federal judges appointed for life, had the power to interpret the Constitution, they would do so "at their peril"; if the people disapproved the interpretation, they "could remove them" ("Brutus," No. 15). The ideal went beyond a close control of officials by the people. In a truly self-governing society, there would be such dialogue, empathy, and even intimacy that the very distinction between ruler and ruled would tend to disappear. Such a close link between the people and officials would embody the idea of liberty being both security of rights and effective voice in public affairs. The anti-federalists groped for mechanisms that would give reality to this idea: how could it be achieved, in substance as well as in form, in a large nation?

For anti-federalists the bonds between the people and their representatives had to be trustworthy as well as close. Not only, as Melancton Smith put it, should "representatives resemble those they represent," but they should possess especially the virtues most characteristic of ordinary people: they should be temperate, moral, and of restrained ambition. Smith acknowledged that "the same passions and prejudices govern all men," but it was also true that "circumstances…give a cast to human character." The wealthy and the powerful, sad to say, were inclined to cheat customers, disdain honest labor, raise armies, put on social airs, and oppress the people. Could they be expected to rule wisely and justly in the interests of all? Rather, it was necessary that people of the "middling sort," average people, perhaps yeoman farmers, themselves take part in government—even be elected to office in large enough numbers to "set the tone" in the capital. Such people, in the daily round of their occupations, Smith observed, had "less temptations, [and] are inclined by habit, and by the company with whom they associate, to set bounds to their passions and appetites." He envisioned, then, a government of popular confidence and respect, vital at the local levels where the virtues of ordinary people could prevail. Though Smith articulated this more forthrightly than most anti-federalists, many others expressed the ideal implicitly (see "John DeWitt," Patrick Henry, and "the Federal Farmer"), and it was consistent with a moral and civic tradition long familiar in the Western world.

This was idealistic, of course, but the anti-federalists thought the goal of the American Revolution was to end the ancient equation of power where arrogant, oppressive, and depraved rulers on one side produced subservience and a gradual erosion of the self-respect, capacities, and virtue of the people on the other side. The result was an increasing corruption and degeneracy in both rulers and ruled. Unless this cycle could be broken, Independence would mean little more than the exchange of one tyranny for another. The aspirations of the federalists for commercial growth, westward expansion, increased national power, and effective world diplomacy were in some ways attractive and worthy, but they also fitted an ominous, all too familiar pattern of "great, splendid,…consolidated government" and "Universal Empire" that the American Revolution had been fought to eradicate. Many anti-federalists, inchoately perhaps, were unwilling to abandon this ideal and the hope that the New World might be a different and better place to live.

The ratification contest, then, was at bottom a debate over the future of the nation. Beneath the disputes about detailed clauses were deep differences over what fulfillment of the American Revolution meant. To the federalists, it meant independence, growth in national power, and prosperity, all within a federal system of government retaining the states and deriving its authority from the people, but also competent to all the needs and exigencies of respectable, energetic nationhood. This was an attractive purpose for large numbers of people of all classes and was in their view a legitimate outgrowth of the Revolution. The anti-federalists, on the other hand, sought a society where virtuous, hardworking honest men and women lived simply in their own communities, enjoyed their families and their neighbors, were devoted to the common welfare, and had such churches, schools, trade associations, and local governments as they needed to sustain their values and purposes. Though this intention was seldom fully or clearly articulated, it permeates anti-federalist writing enough to reveal what their positive ideal was. The quick adoption of the Bill of Rights, the ready acceptance of the new constitution by former anti-federalists, and the Jeffersonian triumph of 1801 with its manifold anti-federalist overtones, all attest to the vigor and influence of anti-federalism and its ability to find fulfillment even under the document opposed so vehemently in 1787-1788. Antifederal ideas have also surfaced again and again in various guises among later generations of Americans. Those ideas, as well as the enticing prospects held out by Publius, are a vital element in the American political tradition and are properly viewed as part of the philosophy of the Constitution.

—RALPH KETCHAM
Syracuse University

Arrangement, Use, and Editing of the Documents

This book, along with the Signet Classics edition of *The Federalist Papers*, presents the context of political ideas within which the Federal Constitution of 1787 came into being. The selections from the debates at the Federal Convention of 1787 (almost entirely from Madison's Notes) have been made to emphasize basic expositions, disagreements, and stages of development of the Constitution. Thus, such major representations at the Convention as William Paterson's proposals and speech of June 15, Hamilton's speech of the 18th, and Madison's of June 6 and June 19 are printed in full. Selections from the ratification controversy are not necessarily the best known or most influential contributions to the debate but rather have been chosen for the cogency of their political thought. In most cases, full speeches, exchanges in debate, and essays are printed, rather than excerpts. Largely neglected are explanations of votes on specific issues, the various practical compromises that influenced the shape of the final document, and ratification pieces concentrating on particular economic or regional disputes. There is no effort, then, to explain or document either the Convention of 1787 or the ratification process as political events, though they surely were such and have been described and analyzed often by historians in that way (see bibliography). Readers will find in this volume and in *The Federalist Papers* the most profound and enduring political thought evoked by the drafting and ratification of the world's oldest still-in-use constitution.

Used with the Signet Classics edition of *The Federalist Papers*, this book gives scholars and students access to the major expositions of and arguments over the Federal Constitution of 1787. Throughout the general introduction and the notes for particular documents, cross-references are made to related or contrasting numbers of *The Federalist Papers*. A table on p. xxxix lists opposing federalist and anti-federalist writings on major topics. The index of ideas in this volume uses the same topics as appear in the "Index of Ideas" in the Signet Classics editon of *The Federalist Papers* to facilitate comparisons of thought in the Convention debates, in *The Federalist Papers* and in anti-federalist writings. This volume is thus designed to be an easy-to-use companion to *The Federalist Papers* by offering from the other major sources on the Constitution parallel or equivalent expressions of political thought.

The editor's "long list" of the best *Federalist* papers would include Numbers 1, 2, 3, 6, 9, 10, 14, 15, 23, 27, 30, 37, 39, 45, 49, 51, 52, 53, 57, 62, 63, 66, 67, 68, 69, 70, 73, 76, 78, and 84. A shorter list of the most important *Federalist* essays would include only Numbers 1, 2, 6, 10, 14, 23, 39, 45, 51, 57, 62, 70, 78, and 84. Clinton Rossiter, editor of the Signet Classics *Federalist*, lists Numbers 1, 2, 6, 9, 10, 14, 15, 16, 23, 37, 39, 47, 48, 49, 51, 62, 63, 70, 78, 84, and 85 as "the cream of the eighty-five papers." Readers wanting to read or teachers having time to assign only part of *The Federalist Papers* can be guided by these selected lists, or make their own abridgements.

Two documents beyond selections from the Convention debates and anti-federalist writings are included. First, James Madison's letter to George Washington of April 16, 1787, outlining what would become known as the Virginia Plan, is reprinted as a general introduction to the work of the Federal Convention. Second, James Wilson's speech of October 6, 1787, the most complete, visible, and widely commented-on early defense of the Constitution, is reprinted because it was the target, direct or indirect, of much of the anti-federalist criticism reprinted in this volume. More than *The Federalist Papers* (or any of its authors, who were unidentified in 1787-1788), Wilson was the chief public advocate of the Constitution. His speech holds an especially important place, theoretically and practically, in the ratification contest.

The selections from the Convention debates are in chronological order with titles added to indicate in general the focus of any particular excerpt. Debate among several Convention delegates is often included when the exchanges reveal opposing arguments on basic points. Editorial apparatus indicates briefly the place of each document in the ratification debate, identifies (where possible) its author, and states the time and place of first delivery and/or printing. The selections from anti-federalist writings are grouped according to their place in the evolution of the fundamental theoretical controversy. That is, documents questioning whether a more energetic central government was needed in 1787 come first (the starting place for the debate over the proposed constitution), those asserting the tyrannical tendencies of the more energetic frame of government come next, and those explicating an emerging anti-federalist idea of government by consent come last. Though this arrangement imposes some order that would perhaps not have been evident in 1787-1788, it is intended to help students understand the most important theoretical issues of the debate. Since the date of first delivery or publication of each selection is indicated, easy reference to them in chronological order is possible (see chronology, pp. xxxvi-xxxviii).

In some cases, punctuation, italics, and spellings likely to confuse twentieth-century readers have been corrected to conform to modern usage. Brackets in the printed sources indicating slight variations in texts have been removed, and most abbreviations have been spelled out, to enhance readability. Ellipses indicate short deletion of words. In general, care has been taken to ensure fidelity to the original text and to remove obstacles to easy reading for modern students.

ACKNOWLEDGMENTS

The editor gratefully acknowledges the support of the John Ben Snow Foundation in preparing the manuscript, and the advice of the staff of the Institute of Early American History and Culture on editorial matters.

List of Plans, Proposals, and Amendments

1. Madison's Pre-Convention outline to Washington, April 16, 1787
2. The Virginia Plan, May 29, 1787
3. The New Jersey Plan, June 15, 1787
4. Hamilton's Plan for National Government, June 18, 1787
5. First Draft of the Constitution, August 6, 1787
6. Amendments Proposed by Pennsylvania Anti-federalists, December 18, 1787
7. Amendments Proposed by Massachusetts and Virginia Anti-federalists, February 7 and June 27, 1788
8. The Articles of Confederation, March 1, 1781
9. The Federal Constitution, September 17, 1787

Chronology of Documents and Important Events

1781: March 1 – Articles of Confederation become effective

1786: Sept. 14 – Annapolis Convention calls for a Convention of all the states

1787: Feb. 21 – Continental Congress calls a Convention in Philadelphia to revise the Articles of Confederation

April 16 – Letter, Madison to Washington, outlining the "Virginia Plan" (p. 3)

May 25 – Constitutional Convention begins in Philadelphia

May 29 – Randolph presents the "Virginia Plan" (p. 7)

June 15 – Paterson presents the "New Jersey Plan" (p. 39)

June 18 – Hamilton presents plan for national government (p. 48)

July 16 – "Great Compromise" adopted

August 6 – First Draft of Constitution (p. 122)

Sept. 17 – Constitution approved, Convention adjourns (p. 177)

Oct. 5 – "Centinel" No. 1 (p. 232)

Oct. 6 – Speech of James Wilson, supporting the Constitution (p. 181)

Oct. 8 – "Federal Farmer" No. 1 (p. 266)

Oct. 9 – "Federal Farmer" No. 2 (p. 276)

Oct. 18 – "Brutus" No. 1 (p. 281)

Oct. 22 – "John DeWitt" No. 1 (p. 188)

Oct. 27 – "John DeWitt" No. 2 (p. 194); Federalist No. 1

Oct. 31 – Federalist No. 2

Nov. 5 – "John DeWitt" No. 3 (p. 329)

Nov. 14 – Federalist No. 6

Nov. 22 – Federalist No. 10

Nov. 22 – "Cato" No. 5 (p. 336)

Nov. 29 – "Brutus" No. 4 (p. 345)

Nov. 30 – Federalist No. 14

Dec. 7 – Delaware ratifies (30-0)

Dec. 12 – Pennsylvania ratifies (46-23)

Dec. 18 – New Jersey ratifies (39-0); Federalist No. 23; Address of Pennsylvania Minority (p. 243)

Dec. 27 – "Brutus" No. 6 (p. 293)

1788: Jan. 2 – Georgia ratifies (26-0)

Jan. 3 – "Cato" No. 7 (p. 341)

Jan. 9 – Connecticut ratifies (128-40)

Jan. 16 – Federalist No. 39

Jan. 24 – "Brutus" No. 10 (p. 302)

Jan. 26 – Federalist No. 45

Jan. 31 – "Brutus" No. 11 (p. 308)

Feb. 6 – Federalist No. 51; Massachusetts ratifies (187-168)

Feb. 7 – "Brutus" No. 12 (p. 315); Massachusetts proposed amendments (p. 220)

Feb. 14 – "Brutus" No. 12 (Part II) (p. 319)

Feb. 19 – Federalist No. 57

Feb. 27 – Federalist No. 62

March 15 – Federalist No. 70

March 20 – "Brutus" No. 15 (p. 322)

April 10 – "Brutus" No. 16 (p. 353)

April 26 – Maryland ratifies (63-11)

May 23 – South Carolina ratifies (149-73)

May 28 – Federalist Nos. 78 and 84

June 5 and 7 – Patrick Henry speeches opposing ratification in Virginia (p. 199)

June 21 – New Hampshire ratifies (57-47); the ninth state

June 20-27 – Melancton Smith speeches opposing ratification in New York (p. 358)

June 25 – Virginia ratifies (89-79)

June 27 – Virginia proposes amendments (p. 222)

July 26 – New York ratifies (30-27)

August 4 – North Carolina rejects ratification (193-75)

1789: March 4 – Constitution takes effect

June 8 – Madison introduces amendments for a Bill of Rights in Congress

Nov. 21 – North Carolina ratifies (195-77)

1790: May 29 – Rhode Island ratifies (34-32)

1791: Nov. 3 – Bill of Rights (Amendments 1-10) takes effect

Summary of Opposed Arguments in Federalist and Anti-federalist Writings

Subject	Anti-federalist Writing	[opposes] Federalist
Need for Stronger Union	John Dewitt # I & II	Federalist # 1-6
Bill of Rights	John Dewitt # II	James Wilson, 10/6/87 Federalist # 84
Nature and Powers of the Union	Patrick Henry, 6/5/88	Federalist # 1, 14, 15
Responsibility and Checks in Self-government	Centinel # I	Federalist # 10, 51
Extent of Union, States' Rights, Bill of Rights, Taxation	Pennsylvania Minority; Brutus # I	Federalist # 10, 32, 33, 35, 36, 39, 45, 84
Extended Republics, Taxation	Federal Farmer # I & II	Federalist # 8, 10, 14, 35, 36
Broad Construction, Taxing Powers	Brutus # VI	Federalist # 23, 30-34
Defense, Standing Armies	Brutus # X	Federalist # 24-29
The Judiciary	Brutus # XI, XII, XV	Federalist # 78-83
Government Resting on the People	John DeWitt # III	Federalist # 23, 49
Executive Power	Cato # V	Federalist # 67
Regulating Elections	Cato # VII	Federalist # 59
House of Representatives	Brutus # IV	Federalist # 27, 28, 52-54, 57
The Senate	Brutus # XVI	Federalist # 62, 63
Representation in House of Representatives and Senate	Melancton Smith, 6/20-6/27/88	Federalist # 52-57, 62, 63

PART I

THE FEDERAL CONVENTION OF 1787

James Madison to George Washington (April 16, 1787)

Even before the final ratification and implementation of the Articles of Confederation on March 1, 1781, many political leaders had challenged them. Those with heavy responsibility for conducting the war against Great Britain, including George Washington, Robert Morris, and Alexander Hamilton, believed the Articles were inadequate to the needs of national government. Many who had long served in the Continental Congress, including James Madison, Thomas Jefferson, and James Wilson, became convinced that that body was ill-conceived to provide effective, republican government. When quarrels among the states, stalemate in Congress, domestic disturbances, foreign intrigue, and commercial disarray clouded public affairs during the 1780s, thoughtful people increasingly advocated a change in the frame of government.

Foremost among such advocates was James Madison, whose service in Congress, 1780-1783, had convinced him that a stronger national government was needed. As a Virginia legislator, 1784-1786, he worked toward that end, and he supported the Mount Vernon meeting of 1785 and the Annapolis Convention of 1786 as steps in the right direction. He also undertook systematic study of "Ancient and Modern Confederacies" to glean ideas for improving the American confederacy. Most pointedly, he examined "The Political System of the United States" to identify its "Vices," as he put it. When it became clear in the winter of 1786-1787 that a new convention of the states would gather in Philadelphia in May 1787, Madison digested his general thoughts into a plan for a new frame of government, for the benefit of his colleagues in the Virginia delegation. He formulated the proposals offered to the convention by Edmund Randolph as the "Virginia Plan," and he wrote to George Washington, on April 16, 1787, explaining the flaws in the Articles of Confederation and the changes that would be needed to give the nation effective government. This letter was first printed in 1840, and is reprinted here from G. Hunt and J. B. Scott, eds., The Debates of the Federal Convention of 1787 (New York, 1920), pp. 592-595.

I have been honoured with your letter of the 31 of March, and find with much pleasure that your views of the reform which ought to be pursued by the Convention, give a sanction to those which I have entertained. Temporising applications will dishonor the Councils which propose them, and may foment the internal malignity of the disease, at the same time that they produce an ostensible palliation of it. Radical attempts, although unsuccessful, will at least justify the authors of them.

Having been lately led to revolve the subject which is to undergo the discussion of the Convention, and formed in my mind *some* outlines of a new system, I take the liberty of submitting them without apology, to your eye.

Conceiving that an individual independence of the States is utterly irreconcilable with their aggregate sovereignty; and that a consolidation of the whole into one simple republic would be as inexpedient as it is unattainable, I have sought for some middle ground, which may at once support a due supremacy of the national authority, and not exclude the local authorities wherever they can be subordinately useful.

I would propose as the ground-work that a change be made in the principle of representation. According to the present form of the Union in which the intervention of the States is in all great cases necessary to effectuate the measures of Congress, an equality of suffrage, does not destroy the inequality of importance, in the several members. No one will deny that Virginia and Massachusetts have more weight and influence both within and without Congress than Delaware or Rhode Island. Under a system which would operate in many essential points without the intervention of the State Legislatures, the ease would be materially altered. A vote in the national Councils from Delaware, would then have the same effect and value as one from the largest State in the Union. I am ready to believe that such a change will not be attended with much difficulty. A majority of the States, and those of greatest influence, will regard it as favorable to them. To the Northern States it will be recommended by their present populousness; to the Southern by their expected advantage in this respect. The lesser States must in every event yield to the predominant will. But the consideration which particularly urges a change in the representation is that it will obviate the principal objections of the larger States to the necessary concessions of power.

I would propose next that in addition to the present federal powers, the national Government should be armed with positive and compleat authority in all cases which require uniformity; such as the regulation of trade, including the right of taxing both exports and imports, the fixing the terms and forms of naturalization, *etc. etc.*

Over and above this positive power, a negative *in all cases whatsoever* on the legislative acts of the States, as heretofore exercised by the Kingly prerogative, appears to me to be absolutely necessary, and to be the least possible encroachment on the State jurisdictions. Without this defensive power, every positive power that can be given on paper will be evaded and defeated. The States will continue to invade the National jurisdiction to violate treaties and the law of nations and to harass each other with rival and spiteful measures dictated by mistaken views of interest. Another happy effect of this prerogative would be its controul on the internal vicisitudes of State policy, and the aggressions of interested majorities on the rights of minorities and of individuals. The great desideratum which has not yet been found for Republican Governments seems to be some disinterested and dispassionate umpire in disputes between different passions and interests in the State. The majority who alone have the right of decision, have frequently an interest real or supposed in abusing it. In Monarchies the sovereign is more neutral to the interests and views of different parties; but, unfortunately he too often forms interests of his own repugnant to those of the whole. Might not the national prerogative here suggested be found sufficiently disinterested for the decision of local questions of policy, whilst it would itself be sufficiently restrained from the pursuit of interests adverse to those of the whole Society? There has not been any moment since the peace at which the representatives of the Union would have given an assent to paper money or any other measure of a kindred nature.

The national supremacy ought also to be extended as I conceive to the Judiciary departments. If those who are to expound and apply the laws, are connected by their interests and their oaths with the particular States wholly, and not with the Union, the participation of the Union in the making of the laws may be possibly rendered unavailing. It seems at least necessary that the oaths of the Judges should include a fidelity to the general as well as local constitution, and that an appeal should lie to some National tribunals in all cases to which foreigners or inhabitants of other States may be parties. The admiralty jurisdiction seems to fall entirely within the purview of the national Government.

The national supremacy in the Executive departments is liable to some difficulty, unless the officers administering them could be made appointable by the supreme Government. The Militia ought certainly to be placed in some form or other under the authority which is entrusted with the general protection and defence.

A Government composed of such extensive power should be well organised and balanced. The legislative department might be divided into two branches; one of them chosen every years by the people at large, or by the Legislatures; the other to consist of fewer members, to hold their places for a longer term, and to go out in such a rotation as always to leave in office a large majority of old members. Perhaps the negative on the laws might be most conveniently exercised by this branch. As a further check, a council of revision including the great ministerial officers might be super-added.

A National Executive must also be provided. I have scarcely ventured as yet to form my own opinion either of the manner in which it ought to be constituted or of the authorities with which it ought to be cloathed.

An article should be inserted expressly guarantying the tranquility of the States against internal as well as external dangers.

In like manner the right of coercion should be expressly declared. With the resources of Commerce in hand, the National administration might always find means of exerting it either by sea or land. But the difficulty and awkwardness of operating by force on the collective will of a State, render it particularly desireable that the necessity of it might be precluded. Perhaps the negative on the laws might create such a mutuality of dependence between the General and particular authorities, as to answer this purpose or perhaps some defined objects of taxation might be submitted along with commerce, to the general authority.

To give a new System its proper validity and energy, a ratification must be obtained from the people, and not merely from the ordinary authority of the Legislatures. This will be the more essential as inroads on the *existing Constitutions* of the States will be unavoidable....

The Virginia Plan (May 29)

The debates of the Convention began on May 29, when Governor Edmund Randolph of Virginia laid before it the plan of government Madison had outlined to Washington the month before and which the entire Virginia delegation had discussed and agreed to as they waited for other delegates to arrive. The plan embodied Madison's intention to greatly strengthen the national government, and boldly set out to frame an entirely new constitution rather than simply amend the Articles of Confederation as the Convention was formally charged to do. The "Virginia Plan," as it came to be called, became the agenda for the Convention as its provisions were debated, amended, and voted on in the succeeding weeks. Randolph's introductory remarks and the Virginia Plan follow in full from Madison's notes taken while the Convention was in session and recorded in the third person (all subsequent excerpts from the debates are also from Madison's Notes, unless indicated otherwise). They are reprinted here from the relevant portions of Documents Illustrative of the Formation of the Union of the American States *(Government Printing Office, Washington, DC, 1927), ed. by C. C. Tansill, pp.114-745.*

MR. RANDOLPH expressed his regret, that it should fall to him, rather than those, who were of longer standing in life and political experience, to open the great subject of their mission. But, as the convention had originated from Virginia, and his colleagues supposed that some proposition was expected from them, they had imposed this task on him.

He then commented on the difficulty of the crisis, and the necessity of preventing the fulfillment of the prophecies of the American downfall.

He observed that in revising the federal system we ought to inquire 1) into the properties, which such a government ought to possess, 2) the defects of the confederation, 3) the danger of our situation and 4) the remedy.

1. The Character of such a government ought to secure 1) against foreign invasion: 2) against dissentions between members of the Union, or seditions in particular states: 3) to procure to the several States, various blessings, of which an isolated situation was incapable: 4) to be able to defend itself against incroachment: and 5) to be paramount to the state constitutions.

2. In speaking of the defects of the confederation he professed a high respect for its authors, and considered them, as having done all that patriots could do, in

the then infancy of the science, of constitutions, and of confederacies,—when the inefficiency of requisitions was unknown—no commercial discord had arisen among any states—no rebellion had appeared as in Massachusetts—foreign debts had not become urgent—the havoc of paper money had not been foreseen—treaties had not been violated—and perhaps nothing better could be obtained from the jealousy of the states with regard to their sovereignty.

He then proceeded to enumerate the defects: 1) That the confederation produced no security against foreign invasion; congress not being permitted to prevent a war nor to support it by their own authority—Of this he cited many examples; most of which tended to show, that they could not cause infractions of treaties or of the law of nations, to be punished: that particular states might by their conduct provoke war without control; and that neither militia nor draughts being fit for defence on such occasions, inlistments only could be successful, and these could not be executed without money. 2) That the federal government could not check the quarrels between states, nor a rebellion in any, not having constitutional power nor means to interpose according to the exigency. 3) That there were many advantages, which the U. S. might acquire, which were not attainable under the confederation—such as a productive impost—counteraction of the commercial regulations of other nations—pushing of commerce ad libitum—etc. *etc.* 4) That the federal government could not defend itself against the incroachments from the states. 5) That it was not even paramount to the state constitutions, ratified, as it was in many of the states.

3. He next reviewed the danger of our situation, appealed to the sense of the best friends of the United States—the prospect of anarchy from the laxity of government everywhere; and to other considerations.

4. He then proceeded to the remedy; the basis of which he said must be the republican principle.

He proposed as conformable to his ideas the following resolutions, which he explained one by one.

Resolutions Proposed by Mr. Randolph in Convention

1. Resolved that the Articles of Confederation ought to be so corrected and enlarged as to accomplish the objects proposed by their institution; namely, "common defense, security of liberty and general welfare."

2. Resolved therefore that the rights of suffrage in the National Legislature ought to be proportioned to the Quotas of contribution, or to the number of free inhabitants, as the one or the other rule may seem best in different cases.

3. Resolved that the National Legislature ought to consist of two branches.

4. Resolved that the members of the first branch of the National Legislature ought to be elected by the people of the several States every for the term of; to be of the age of years at least, to receive liberal stipends by which they may be compensated for the devotion of their time to public service; to be ineligible to any office established by a particular State, or under the authority of the United States, except those peculiarly belonging to the functions of the first branch, during the term of service, and for the space of after its expiration; to be incapable of re-election for the space of after the expiration of their term of service, and to be subject to recall.

5. Resolved that the members of the second branch of the National Legislature ought to be elected by those of the first, out of a proper number of persons nominated by the individual Legislatures, to be of the age of years at least; to hold their offices for a term sufficient to ensure their independency; to receive liberal stipends, by which they may be compensated for the devotion of their time to public service; and to be ineligible to any office established by a particular State, or under the authority of the United States, except those peculiarly belonging to the functions of the second branch, during the term of service, and for the space of after the expiration thereof.

6. Resolved that each branch ought to possess the right of originating Acts; that the National Legislature ought to be impowered to enjoy the Legislative Rights vested in Congress by the Confederation and moreover to legislate in all cases to which the separate States are incompetent, or in which the harmony of the United States may be interrupted by the exercise of individual Legislation; to negative all laws passed by the several States, contravening in the opinion of the National Legislature the articles of Union; and to call forth the force of the Union against any member of the Union failing to fulfill its duty under the articles thereof.

7. Resolved that a National Executive be instituted; to be chosen by the National Legislature for the term of years to receive punctually at stated times, a fixed compensation for the services rendered, in which no increase or diminution shall be made so as to affect the Magistracy, existing at the time of increase or diminution, and to be ineligible a second time; and that besides a general authority to execute the National laws, it ought to enjoy the Executive rights vested in Congress by the Confederation.

8. Resolved that the Executive and a convenient number of the National Judiciary, ought to compose a Council of revision with authority to examine every act of the National Legislature before it shall operate, and every act of a particular Legislature before a Negative thereon shall be final; and that the dissent of the said Council shall amount to a rejection, unless the Act of the National Legislature be again passed, or that of a particular Legislature be again

National Legislature be again passed, or that of a particular Legislature be again negatived by of the members of each branch.

9. Resolved that a National Judiciary be established to consist of one or more supreme tribunals, and of inferior tribunals to be chosen by the National Legislature, to hold their offices during good behaviour; and to receive punctually at stated times fixed compensation for their services, in which no increase or diminution shall be made so as to affect the persons actually in office at the time of such increase or diminution. That the jurisdiction of the inferior tribunals shall be to hear and determine in the first instance, and of the supreme tribunal to hear and determine in the [last] resort, all piracies and felonies on the high seas, captures from an enemy; cases in which foreigners or citizens of other States applying to such jurisdictions may be interested, or which respect the collection of the National revenue; impeachments of any National officers, and questions which may involve the national peace and harmony.

10. Resolved that provision ought to be made for the admission of States lawfully arising within the limits of the United States, whether from a voluntary junction of Government and Territory or otherwise, with the consent of a number of voices in the National Legislature less than the whole.

11. Resolved that a Republican Government and the territory of each State, except in the instance of a voluntary junction of Government and territory, ought to be guaranteed by the United States to each State.

12. Resolved that provision ought to be made for the continuance of Congress and their authorities and privileges, until a given day after the reform of the articles of Union shall be adopted, and for the completion of all their engagements.

13. Resolved that provision ought to be made for the amendment of the Articles of Union whensoever it shall seem necessary, and that the assent of the National Legislature ought not to be required thereto.

14. Resolved that the Legislative, Executive and Judiciary powers within the several States ought to be bound by oath to support the articles of Union.

15. Resolved that the amendments which shall be offered to the Confederation, by the Convention ought at a proper time, or times, after the approbation of Congress to be submitted to an assembly or assemblies of Representatives, recommended by the several Legislatures to be expressly chosen by the people, to consider and decide thereon.

He concluded with an exhortation, not to suffer the present opportunity of establishing general peace, harmony, happiness and liberty in the U. S. to pass away unimproved.

Debate on Representation (May 31)

The Convention first took up the clause in the Virginia Plan calling for the members of the House of Representatives to be elected directly by the people of the several states. The debate revealed basically divergent attitudes toward rule by the people.

    Mr. Sherman opposed the election by the people, insisting that it ought to be by the State Legislatures. The people he said, immediately should have as little to do as may be about the Government. They want information and are constantly liable to be misled.

    Mr. Gerry. The evils we experience flow from the excess of democracy. The people do not want virtue, but are the dupes of pretended patriots. In Massachusetts it had been fully confirmed by experience that they are daily misled into the most baneful measures and opinions by the false reports circulated by designing men, and which no one on the spot can refute. One principal evil arises from the want of due provision for those employed in the administration of Government. It would seem to be a maxim of democracy to starve the public servants. He mentioned the popular clamour in Massachusetts for the reduction of salaries and the attack made on that of the Governor though secured by the spirit of the Constitution itself. He had he said been too republican heretofore: he was still however republican, but had been taught by experience the danger of the levolling spirit.

    Mr. Mason argued strongly for an election of the larger branch by the people. It was to be the grand depository of the democratic principle of the government. It was, so to speak, to be our House of Commons—It ought to know and sympathize with every part of the community; and ought therefore to be taken not only from different parts of the whole republic, but also from different districts of the larger members of it, which had in several instances particularly in Virginia different interests and views arising from difference of produce, of habits etc., *etc.* He admitted that we had been too democratic but was afraid we should incautiously run into the opposite extreme. We ought to attend to the rights of every class of the people. He had often wondered at the indifference of the superior classes of society to this dictate of humanity and policy; considering that however affluent their circumstances, or elevated their situations, might be, the course of a few years, not only might but certainly would, distribute their posterity throughout the lowest classes of Society. Every selfish motive therefore, every family attachment, ought to recommend such a system of policy as would provide no less carefully for the rights and happiness of the lowest than of the highest orders of Citizens.

MR. WILSON contended strenuously for drawing the most numerous branch of the Legislature immediately from the people. He was for raising the federal pyramid to a considerable altitude, and for that reason wished to give it as broad a basis as possible. No government could long subsist without the confidence of the people. In a republican Government this confidence was peculiarly essential. He also thought it wrong to increase the weight of the State Legislatures by making them the electors of the National Legislature. All interference between the general and local governments should be obviated as much as possible. On examination it would be found that the opposition of States to federal measures had preceded much more from the officers of the States, than from the people at large.

MR. MADISON considered the popular election of one branch of the National Legislature as essential to every plan of free Government. He observed that in some of the States one branch of the Legislature was composed of men already removed from the people by an intervening body of electors. That if the first branch of the general legislature should be elected by the State Legislatures, the second branch elected by the first—the Executive by the second together with the first; and other appointments again made for subordinate purposes by the Executive, the people would be lost sight of altogether; and the necessary sympathy between them and their rulers and officers, too little felt. He was an advocate for the policy of refining the popular appointments by successive filtrations, but thought it might be pushed too far. He wished the expedient to be resorted to only in the appointment of the second branch of the Legislature, and in the Executive and judiciary branches of the Government. He thought too that the great fabric to be raised would be more stable and durable, if it should rest on the solid foundation of the people themselves, than if it should stand merely on the pillars of the Legislatures.

MR. GERRY did not like the election by the people. The maxims taken from the British constitution were often fallacious when applied to our situation which was extremely different. Experience he said had shown that the State legislatures drawn immediately from the people did not always possess their confidence. He had no objection however to an election by the people if it were so qualified that men of honor and character might not be unwilling to be joined in the appointments. He seemed to think the people might nominate a certain number out of which the State Legislatures should be bound to choose.

Debate on Executive Power (June 1)

The Convention next considered the clause providing for a national executive. Since the Articles of Confederation had not provided for executive power, and since revolutionary hostility to the executive power of the British monarchy remained strong, members were unusually hesitant about fashioning such an unprecedented and potentially oppressive office.

MR. PINCKNEY was for a vigorous Executive but was afraid the Executive powers of the existing Congress might extend to peace and war and etc., etc., which would render the Executive a monarchy, of the worst kind, to wit an elective one.

MR. WILSON moved that the Executive consist of a single person. Mr. C. PINCKNEY seconded the motion, so as to read "that a National Executive to consist of a single person, be instituted."

A considerable pause ensuing and the Chairman asking if he should put the question, Dr. FRANKLIN observed that it was a point of great importance and wished that the gentlemen would deliver their sentiments on it before the question was put.

MR. RUTLEDGE animadverted on the shyness of gentlemen on this and other subjects. He said it looked as if they supposed themselves precluded by having frankly disclosed their opinions from afterwards changing them, which he did not take to be at all the case. He said he was for vesting the Executive power in a single person, though he was not for giving him the power of war and peace. A single man would feel the greatest responsibility and administer the public affairs best.

MR. SHERMAN said he considered the Executive magistracy as nothing more than an institution for carrying the will of the Legislature into effect, that the person or persons ought to be appointed by and accountable to the Legislature only, which was the depository of the supreme will of the Society. As they were the best judges of the business which ought to be done by the Executive department, and consequently of the number necessary from time to time for doing it, he wished the number might not be fixed, but that the Legislature should be at liberty to appoint one or more as experience might dictate.

MR. WILSON preferred a single magistrate, as giving most energy dispatch and responsibility to the office. He did not consider the Prerogatives of the

British Monarch as a proper guide in defining the Executive powers. Some of these prerogatives were of a Legislative nature. Among others that of war and peace etc., *etc.* The only powers he conceived strictly Executive were those of executing the laws, and appointing officers, not appertaining to and appointed by the Legislature.

Mr. Gerry favored the policy of annexing a Council to the Executive in order to give weight and inspire confidence.

Mr. Randolph strenuously opposed a unity in the Executive magistracy. He regarded it as the fetus of monarchy. We had he said no motive to be governed by the British Government as our prototype. He did not mean however to throw censure on that Excellent fabric. If we were in a situation to copy it he did not know that he should be opposed to it; but the fixed genius of the people of America required a different form of Government. He could not see why the great requisites for the Executive department, vigor, despatch and responsibility could not be found in three men, as well as in one man. The Executive ought to be independent. It ought therefore in order to support its independence to consist of more than one.

Mr. Wilson said that unity in the Executive instead of being the fetus of monarchy would be the best safeguard against tyranny. He repeated that he was not governed by the British Model which was inapplicable to the situation of this Country; the extent of which was so great, and the manners so republican, that nothing but a great confederated Republic would do for it.

Opposition to Executive Salaries (June 2)

As the Convention further inconclusively considered the executive department, Benjamin Franklin spoke on behalf of a favorite idea of his: that officers of government should not receive salaries.

    It is with reluctance that I rise to express a disapprobation of any one article of the plan for which we are so much obliged to the honorable gentleman who laid it before us. From its first reading I have borne a good will to it, and in general wished it success. In this particular of salaries to the Executive branch I happen to differ; and as my opinion may appear new and chimerical, it is only from a persuasion that it is right, and from a sense of duty that I hazard it. The Committee will judge of my reasons when they have heard them, and their judgment may possibly change mine—I think I see inconveniences in the appointment of salaries; I see none in refusing them, but on the contrary, great advantages.

    Sir, there are two passions which have a powerful influence on the affairs of men. These are ambition and avarice; the love of power, and the love of money. Separately each of these has great force in prompting men to action; but when united in view of the same object, they have in many minds the most violent effects. Place before the eyes of such men, a post of *honour* that shall be at the same time a place of *profit*, and they will move heaven and earth to obtain it. The vast number of such places it is that renders the British Government so tempestuous. The struggles for them are the true sources of all those factions which are perpetually dividing the Nation, distracting its Councils, hurrying sometimes into fruitless and mischievous wars, and often compelling a submission to dishonorable terms of peace.

    And of what kind are the men that will strive for this profitable pre-eminence, through all the bustle of cabal, the heat of contention, the infinite mutual abuse of parties, tearing to pieces the best of characters? It will not be the wise and moderate; the lovers of peace and good order, the men fittest for the trust. It will be the bold and the violent, the men of strong passions and indefatigable activity in their selfish pursuits. These will thrust themselves into your Government and be your rulers—And these too will be mistaken in the expected happiness of their situation: For their vanquished competitors of the same spirit, and from the same motives will perpetually be endeavouring to distress their administration, thwart their measures, and render them odious to the people.

Besides these evils, Sir, though we may set out in the beginning with moderate salaries, we shall find that such will not be of long continuance. Reasons will never be wanting for proposed augmentations. And there will always be a party for giving more to the rulers, that the rulers may be able in return to give more to them.—Hence as all history informs us, there has been in every State and Kingdom a constant kind of warfare between the governing and governed: the one striving to obtain more for its support, and the other to pay less. And this has alone occasioned great convulsions, actual civil wars, ending either in dethroning of the Princes, or enslaving of the people. Generally indeed the ruling power carries its point, the revenues of princes constantly increasing, and we see that they are never satisfied, but always in want of more. The more the people are discontented with the oppression of taxes; the greater need the prince has of money to distribute among his partizans and pay the troops that are to suppress all resistance, and enable him to plunder at pleasure. There is scarce a king in a hundred who would not, if he could, follow the example of Pharaoh, get first all the people's money, then all their lands, and then make them and their children servants for ever. It will be said, that we don't propose to establish Kings. I know it. But there is a natural inclination in mankind to Kingly Government. It sometimes relieves them from Aristocratic domination. They had rather have one tyrant than five hundred. It gives more of the appearance of equality among Citizens, and that they like. I am apprehensive therefore, perhaps too apprehensive, that the Government of these States, may in future times, end in a Monarchy. But this Catastrophe I think may be long delayed, if in our proposed System we do not sow the seeds of contention, faction and tumult, by making our posts of honor, places of profit. If we do, I fear that though we do employ at first a number, and not a single person, the number will in time be set aside, it will only nourish the fetus of a King, as the honorable gentleman from Virginia very aptly expressed it, and a King will the sooner be set over us.

It may be imagined by some that this is an Utopian Idea, and that we can never find men to serve us in the Executive department, without paying them well for their services. I conceive this to be a mistake. Some existing facts present themselves to me, which incline me to a contrary opinion. The high Sheriff of a County in England is an honorable office, but it is not a profitable one. It is rather expensive and therefore not sought for. But yet, it is executed and well executed, and usually by some of the principal Gentlemen of the

County. In France, the office of Counselor or Member of their Judiciary Parliaments is more honorable. It is therefore purchased at a high price: There are indeed fees on the law proceedings, which are divided among them, but these fees do not amount to more than three percent on the sum paid for the place. Therefore as legal interest is there at five percent they in fact pay two percent for being allowed to do the Judiciary business of the Nation, which is at the same time entirely exempt from the burden of paying them any salaries for their services. I do not however mean to recommend this as an eligible mode for our Judiciary department. I only bring the instance to show that the pleasure of doing good and serving their Country and the respect such conduct entitles them to, are sufficient motives with some minds to give up a great portion of their time to the public, without the mean inducement of pecuniary satisfaction.

Another instance is that of a respectable Society who have made the experiment, and practised it with success more than an hundred years. I mean the Quakers. It is an established rule with them, that they are not to go to law; but in their controversies they must apply to their monthly, quarterly and yearly meetings. Committees of these sit with patience to hear the parties, and spend much time in composing their differences. In doing this, they are supported by a sense of duty, and the respect paid to usefulness. It is honorable to be so employed, but it was never made profitable by salaries, fees, or perquisites. And indeed in all cases of public service the less the profit the greater the honor.

To bring the matter nearer home, have we not seen, the great and most important of our offices, that of General of our armies executed for eight years together without the smallest salary, by a Patriot whom I will not now offend by any other praise; and this through fatigues and distresses in common with the other brave men his military friends and companions, and the constant anxieties peculiar to his station? And shall we doubt finding three or four men in all the United States, with public spirit enough to bear sitting in peaceful Council for perhaps an equal term, merely to preside over our civil concerns, and see that our laws are duly executed? Sir, I have a better opinion of our Country. I think we shall never be without a sufficient number of wise and good men to undertake and execute well and faithfully the office in question.

Sir, the saving of the salaries that may at first be proposed is not an object with me. The subsequent mischiefs of proposing them are what I apprehend. And therefore it is, that I move the amendment. If it is not seconded or accepted I must be contented with the satisfaction of having delivered my opinion frankly and done my duty.

The motion was seconded by COLONEL HAMILTON with the view he said merely of bringing so respectable a proposition before the Committee, and which was besides enforced by arguments that had a certain degree of weight. No debate ensued, and the proposition was postponed for the consideration of the members. It was treated with great respect, but rather for the author of it, than from any apparent conviction of its expediency or practicability.

Opposition to a Unitary Executive (June 4)

Still in an unsettled mood, the Convention again debated the merits of a single vs. a plural executive. George Mason preserved among his papers a copy of a speech opposing a unitary executive. Portions of it are reprinted here from Robert Rutland, ed., The Papers of George Mason *(3 vols., Chapel Hill, NC, 1970), IIII, pp. 896-898.*

The chief advantages which have been urged in favour of Unity in the Executive, are the Secrecy, the Dispatch, the Vigour and Energy which the Government will derive from it; especially in time of War. That these are great Advantages, I shall most readily allow. They have been strongly insisted on by all monarchical Writers—they have been acknowledged by the ablest and most candid Defenders of Republican Government; and it can not be denied that a Monarchy possesses them in a much greater Degree than a Republic. Yet perhaps a little Reflection may incline us to doubt whether these advantages are not greater in Theory than in Practice—or lead us to enquire whether there is not some prevailing Principle in Republican Government, which sets at Naught, and tramples upon this boasted Superiority—as hath been experienced, to their cost by most Monarchys, which have been imprudent enough to invade or attack their republican Neighbors. This invincible Principle is to be found in the Love the Affection the Attachment of the Citizens to their Laws, to their Freedom, and to their Country. Every Husbandman will be quickly converted into a Soldier, when he knows and feels that he is to fight not in defence of the Rights of a particular Family, or a Prince; but for his own. This is the true Construction of that pro Aris and focis [for altars and firesides] which has, in all Ages, perform'd such Wonders. It was this which, in ancient times, enabled the little Cluster of Grecian Republics to resist, and almost constantly to defeat the Persian Monarch. It was this which supported the States of Holland against a Body of veteran Troops through a Thirty Years War with Spain, then the greatest Monarchy in Europe and finally rendered them victorious. It is this which preserves the Freedom and Independence of the Swiss Cantons, in the midst of the most powerful Nations. And who that reflects seriously upon the Situation of America, in the Beginning of the late War—without Arms—without Soldiers—

without Trade, Money, or Credit——in a Manner destitute of all Resources, but must ascribe our Success to this pervading all-powerful Principle?

We have not yet been able to define the Powers of the Executive; and however moderately some Gentlemen may talk or think upon the Subject, I believe there is a general Tendency to a strong Executive and I am inclined to think a strong Executive necessary. If strong and extensive Powers are vested in the Executive, and that Executive consists only of one Person, the Government will of course degenerate, (for I will call it degeneracy) into a Monarchy—A Government so contrary to the Genius of the People, that they will reject even the Appearance of it. I consider the federal Government as in some Measure dissolved by the Meeting of this Convention. Are there no Dangers to be apprehended from procrastinating the time between the breaking up of this Assembly and the adoption of a new System of Government. I dread the Interval. If it should not be brought to an Issue in the Course of the first Year, the Consequences may be fatal. Has not the different Parts of this extensive Government, the several States of which it is composed a Right to expect an equal Participation in the Executive, as the best Means of securing an equal Attention to their Interests. Should an Insurrection, a Rebellion or Invasion happen in New Hampshire when the single supreme Magistrate is a Citizen of Georgia, would not the people of New Hampshire naturally ascribe any Delay in defending them to such a Circumstance and so vice versa. If the Executive is vested in three Persons, one chosen from the northern, one from the middle, and one from the Southern States, will it not contribute to quiet the Minds of the People, & convince them that there will be proper attention paid to their respective Concerns? Will not three Men so chosen bring with them, into Office, a more perfect and extensive Knowledge of the real Interests of this great Union? Will not such a Model of Appointment be the most effectual means of preventing Cabals and Intrigues between the Legislature and the Candidates for this Office, especially with those Candidates who from their local Situation, near the seat of the federal Government, will have the greatest Temptations and the greatest Opportunities. Will it not be the most effectual Means of checking and counteracting the aspiring Views of dangerous and ambitious Men, and consequently the best Security for the Stability and Duration of our Government upon the invaluable Principles of Liberty? These Sir, are some of my Motives for preferring an Executive consisting of three Persons rather than of one.

Electing Representatives (June 6)

After inconclusive discussions of the judiciary and some minor matters, the Convention resumed consideration of the mode of electing the House of Representatives. It debated a motion that the state legislatures, not the people, ought to elect the Representatives.

MR. GERRY. Much depends on the mode of election. In England, the people will probably lose their liberty from the smallness of the proportion having a right of suffrage. Our danger arises from the opposite extreme; hence in Massachusetts the worst men get into the Legislature. Several members of that Body had lately been convicted of infamous crimes. Men of indigence, ignorance and baseness, spare no pains, however dirty to carry their point against men who are superior to the artifices practised. He was not disposed to run into extremes. He was as much principled as ever against aristocracy and monarchy. It was necessary on the one hand that the people should appoint one branch of the government in order to inspire them with the necessary confidence. But he wished the election on the other to be so modified as to secure more effectually a just preference of merit. His idea was that the people should nominate certain persons in certain districts, out of whom the State Legislatures should make the appointment.

MR. WILSON. He wished for vigor in the government but he wished that vigorous authority to flow immediately from the legitimate source of all authority. The government ought to possess not only first the *force*, but secondly the *mind or sense* of the people at large. The Legislature ought to be the most exact transcript of the whole Society. Representation is made necessary only because it is impossible for the people to act collectively. The opposition was to be expected he said from the *Governments*, not from the Citizens of the States. The latter had parted as was observed [by Mr. King] with all the necessary powers, and it was immaterial to them, by whom they were exercised, if well exercised. The State officers were to be the losers of power. The people he supposed would be rather more attached to the national Government than to the State governments as being more important in itself, and more flattering to their pride. There is no danger of improper elections if made by *large* districts. Bad elections proceed from the smallness of the districts which give an opportunity to bad men to intrigue themselves into office.

Mr. Sherman. If it were in view to abolish the State governments, the elections ought to be by the people. If the State governments are to be continued, it is necessary in order to preserve harmony between the National and State governments that the elections to the former should be made by the latter. The right of participating in the National Government would be sufficiently secured to the people by their election of the State Legislatures. The objects of the Union, he thought were few. 1. defence against foreign danger. 2. against internal disputes and a resort to force. 3. treaties with foreign nations. 4. regulating foreign commerce, and drawing revenue from it. These and perhaps a few lesser objects alone rendered a Confederation of the States necessary. All other matters civil and criminal would be much better in the hands of the States. The people are more happy in small than large States. States may indeed be too small as Rhode Island, and thereby be too subject to faction. Some others were perhaps too large, the powers of government not being able to pervade them. He was for giving the General government power to legislate and execute within a defined province.

Colonel Mason. Under the existing Confederacy, congress represents the *States* not the *people* of the States: their acts operate on the *States*, not on the individuals. The case will be changed in the new plan of government. The people will be represented; they ought therefore to choose the Representatives. The requisites in actual representation are that the Representatives should sympathize with their constituents; should think as they think, and feel as they feel; and that for these purposes should even be residents among them. Much he said had been alleged against democratic elections. He admitted that much might be said; but it was to be considered that no Government was free from imperfections and evils; and that improper elections in many instances, were inseparable from Republican Governments. But compare these with the advantage of this Form in favor of the rights of the people, in favor of human nature. He was persuaded there was a better chance for proper elections by the people, if divided into large districts, than by the State Legislatures. Paper money had been issued by the latter when the former were against it. Was it to be supposed that the State Legislatures then would not send to the National Legislature patrons of such projects, if the choice depended on them.

Mr. Madison considered an election of one branch at least of the Legislature by the people immediately, as a clear principle of free government and that this mode under proper regulations had the additional advantage of securing better representatives, as well as of avoiding too great an agency of the State Governments in the General one.—He differed from the member from Connecticut [Mr. Sherman] in thinking the objects mentioned to be all the principal ones that required a National government. Those were certainly important and necessary objects; but he combined with them the necessity of providing more effectually, for the security of private rights, and the steady dispensation of Justice. Interferences with these were evils which had more perhaps than any thing else, produced this convention. Was it to be supposed that republican liberty could long exist under the abuses of it practised in some of the States. The gentleman [Mr. Sherman] had admitted that in a very small State, faction and oppression would prevail. It was to be inferred then that wherever these prevailed the State was too small. Had they not prevailed in the largest as well as the smallest though less than in the smallest; and were we not thence admonished to enlarge the sphere as far as the nature of the government would admit. This was the only defence against the inconveniences of democracy consistent with the democratic form of government. All civilized Societies would be divided into different Sects, Factions, and interests, as they happened to consist of rich and poor, debtors and creditors, the landed, the manufacturing, the commercial interests, the inhabitants of this district or that district, the followers of this political leader or that political leader, the disciples of this religious Sect or that religious Sect. In all cases where a majority are united by a common interest or passion, the rights of the minority are in danger. What motives are to restrain them? A prudent regard to the maxim that honesty is the best policy is found by experience to be as little regarded by bodies of men as by individuals. Respect for character is always diminished in proportion to the number among whom the blame or praise is to be divided. Conscience, the only remaining tie, is known to be inadequate in individuals: In large numbers, little is to be expected from it. Besides, Religion itself may become a motive to persecution and oppression.—These observations are verified by the Histories of every Country ancient and modern. In Greece and Rome the rich and poor, the creditors and debtors, as well as the patricians and plebeians alternately oppressed each other with equal unmercifulness. What a source of oppression was the relation between the parent cities of Rome, Athens and Carthage, and their respective provinces: the former possessing the power, and the latter being sufficiently distinguished to be separate objects of it? Why was America so justly apprehensive of Parliamentary injustice? Because Great Britain had a separate interest real or supposed, and if her authority had been admitted, could have pursued that interest at our expense. We have seen the mere distinction of colour made in the most enlightened period of time, a ground of the most oppressive dominion ever exercised by man over man. What has been the source of those unjust laws complained of among ourselves? Has it not been the real or supposed interest of the major number? Debtors have defrauded their creditors.

The landed interest has borne hard on the mercantile interest. The Holders of one species of property have thrown a disproportion of taxes on the holders of another species. The lesson we are to draw from the whole is that where a majority are united by a common sentiment, and have an opportunity, the rights of the minor party become insecure. In a republican government the Majority if united have always an opportunity. The only remedy is to enlarge the sphere, and thereby divide the community into so great a number of interests and parties, that in the first place a majority will not be likely at the same moment to have a common interest separate from that of the whole or of the minority; and in the second place, that in case they should have such an interest, they may not be apt to unite in the pursuit of it. It was incumbent on us then to try this remedy, and with that view to frame a republican system on such a scale and in such a form as will control all the evils which have been experienced.

MR. DICKINSON considered it as essential that one branch of the Legislature should be drawn immediately from the people; and as expedient that the other should be chosen by the Legislatures of the States. This combination of the State governments with the national government was as politic as it was unavoidable. In the formation of the Senate we ought to carry it through such a refining process as will assimilate it as near as may be to the House of Lords in England. He repeated his warm eulogiums on the British Constitution. He was for a strong National government but for leaving the States a considerable agency in the System. The objection against making the former dependent on the latter might be obviated by giving to the Senate an authority permanent and irrevocable for three, five or seven years. Being thus independent they will speak and decide with becoming freedom.

MR. READ. Too much attachment is betrayed to the State governments. We must look beyond their continuance. A national government must soon of necessity swallow all of them up. They will soon be reduced to the mere office of electing the National Senate. He was against patching up the old federal System: he hoped the idea would be dismissed. It would be like putting new cloth on an old garment. The confederation was founded on temporary principles. It cannot last: it cannot be amended. If we do not establish a good government on new principles, we must either go to ruin, or have the work to do over again. The people at large are wrongly suspected of being averse to a general government. The aversion lies among interested men who possess their confidence.

MR. PIERCE was for an election by the people as to the first branch and by the States as to the second branch; by which means the Citizens of the States would be represented both *individually and collectively*.

Debate on Method of Electing Senators (June 7)

The next day the Convention took up a motion by John Dickinson that the Senate be elected by the state legislatures.

Mr. Sherman seconded the motion; observing that the particular States would thus become interested in supporting the national government and that a due harmony between the two governments would be maintained. He admitted that the two ought to have separate and distinct jurisdictions, but that they ought to have a mutual interest in supporting each other.

Mr. Pinckney. If the small States should be allowed one Senator only, the number will be too great, there will be 80 at least.

Mr. Dickinson had two reasons for his motion. 1. because the sense of the States would be better collected through their Governments than immediately from the people at large; 2. because he wished the Senate to consist of the most distinguished characters, distinguished for their rank in life and their weight of property, and bearing as strong a likeness to the British House of Lords as possible; and he thought such characters more likely to be selected by the State Legislatures, than in any other mode. The greatness of the number was no objection with him. He hoped there would be 80 and twice 80 of them. If their number should be small, the popular branch could not be balanced by them. The legislature of a numerous people ought to be a numerous body.

Mr. Williamson preferred a small number of Senators, but wished that each State should have at least one. He suggested 25 as a convenient number. The different modes of representation in the different branches, will serve as a mutual check.

Mr. Butler was anxious to know the ratio of representation before he gave any opinion.

Mr. Wilson. If we are to establish a national Government, that Government ought to flow from the people at large. If one branch of it should be chosen by the Legislatures, and the other by the people, the two branches will rest on different foundations, and dissensions will naturally arise between them. He wished the Senate to be elected by the people as well as the other branch, and the people might be divided into proper districts for the purpose and moved to postpone the motion of Mr. Dickinson, in order to take up one of that import.

MR. MORRIS seconded him.

MR. READ proposed "that the Senate should be appointed by the Executive Magistrate out of a proper number of persons to be nominated by the individual legislatures." He said he thought it his duty, to speak his mind frankly. Gentlemen he hoped would not be alarmed at the idea. Nothing short of this approach towards a proper model of Government would answer the purpose, and he thought it best to come directly to the point at once.—His proposition was not seconded nor supported.

MR. MADISON. If the motion [of Mr. Dickinson] should be agreed to, we must either depart from the doctrine of proportional representation; or admit into the Senate a very large number of members. The first is inadmissible, being evidently unjust. The second is inexpedient. The use of the Senate is to consist in its proceeding with more coolness, with more system, and with more wisdom, than the popular branch. Enlarge their number and you communicate to them the vices which they are meant to correct. He differed from Mr. D. who thought that the additional number would give additional weight to the body. On the contrary it appeared to him that their weight would be in an inverse ratio to their number. The example of the Roman Tribunes was applicable. They lost their influence and power, in proportion as their number was augmented. The reason seemed to be obvious: They were appointed to take care of the popular interests and pretensions at Rome, because the people by reason of their numbers could not act in concert; were liable to fall into factions among themselves, and to become a prey to their aristocratic adversaries. The more the representatives of the people therefore were multiplied, the more they partook of the infirmities of their constituents, the more liable they became to be divided among themselves either from their own indiscretions or the artifices of the opposite faction, and of course the less capable of fulfilling their trust. When the weight of a set of men depends merely on their personal characters, the greater the number the greater the weight. When it depends on the degree of political authority lodged in them, the smaller the number the greater the weight. These considerations might perhaps be combined in the intended Senate; but the latter was the material one.

MR. GERRY. Four modes of appointing the Senate have been mentioned. 1. By the first branch of the National Legislature. This would create a dependence contrary to the end proposed. 2. By the National Executive. This is a stride towards monarchy that few will think of. 3. By the people. The people have two great interests, the landed interest, and the commercial including the stockholders. To draw both branches from the people will leave no security to the latter interest; the people being chiefly composed of the landed interest, and erroneously supposing, that the other interest are adverse to it. 4. By the Individual Legislatures. The elections being carried through this refinement, will be most likely to provide some check in favor of the commercial interest against the landed; without which oppression will take place, and no free Government can last long where that is the case. He was therefore in favor of this last.

MR. DICKINSON. The preservation of the States in a certain degree of agency is indispensable. It will produce that collision between the different authorities which should be wished for in order to check each other. To attempt to abolish the States altogether, would degrade the Councils of our Country, would be impracticable, would be ruinous. He compared the proposed National System to the Solar System, in which the States were the planets, and ought to be left to move freely in their proper orbits. The Gentleman from Pennsylvania [Mr. Wilson] wished he said to extinguish these planets. If the State Governments were excluded from all agency in the national one, and all power drawn from the people at large, the consequence would be that the national government would move in the same direction as the State governments now do, and would run into all the same mischiefs. The reform would only unite the 13 small streams into one great current pursuing the same course without any opposition whatever. He adhered to the opinion that the Senate ought to be composed of a large number, and that their influence from family weight and other causes would be increased thereby. He did not admit that the Tribunes lost their weight in proportion as their number was augmented and gave a historical sketch of this institution. If the reasoning of [Mr. Madison] was good it would prove that the number of the Senate ought to be reduced below ten, the highest number of the Tribunitial corps.

MR. WILSON. The subject it must be owned is surrounded with doubts and difficulties. But we must surmount them. The British government cannot be our model. We have no materials for a similar one. Our manners, our laws, the abolition of entails and of primo-geniture, the whole genius of the people, are opposed to it. He did not see the danger of the States being devoured by the national government. On the contrary, he wished to keep them from devouring the national government. He was not however for extinguishing these planets as was supposed by Mr. D.—neither did he on the other hand, believe that they would warm or enlighten the Sun. Within their proper orbits they must still be suffered to act for subordinate purposes for which their existence is made essential by the great extent of our Country. He could not comprehend in what manner the landed interest would be rendered less predominant in the Senate, by an election through the medium of the Legislatures than by the people themselves. If the Legislatures, as was now complained, sacrificed the commercial to the landed interest, what reason was there to expect such a choice from them as would defeat their own views. He was for an election by the people in large districts which would be most likely to obtain men of intelligence and uprightness; subdividing the districts only for the accommodation of voters.

Mr. Madison could as little comprehend in what manner family weight, as desired by Mr. D. would be more certainly conveyed into the Senate through elections by the State Legislatures, than in some other modes. The true question was in what mode the best choice would be made? If an election by the people, or through any other channel than the State Legislatures promised as uncorrupt and impartial a preference of merit, there could surely be no necessity for an appointment by those Legislatures. Nor was it apparent that a more useful check would be derived through that channel than from the people through some other. The great evils complained of were that the State Legislatures run into schemes of paper money etc., etc., whenever solicited by the people, and sometimes without even the sanction of the people. Their influence then, instead of checking a like propensity in the National Legislature, may be expected to promote it. Nothing can be more contradictory than to say that the National Legislature without a proper check, will follow the example of the State Legislatures, and in the same breath, that the State Legislatures are the only proper check.

Mr. Sherman opposed elections by the people in districts, as not likely to produce such fit men as elections by the State Legislatures.

Mr. Gerry insisted that the commercial and monied interest would be more secure in the hands of the State Legislatures, than of the people at large. The former have more sense of character, and will be restrained by that from injustice. The people are for paper money when the Legislatures are against it. In Massachusetts the County Conventions had declared a wish for a *depreciating* paper that would sink itself. Besides, in some States there are two Branches in the Legislature, one of which is somewhat aristocratic. There would therefore be so far a better chance of refinement in the choice. There seemed, he thought to be three powerful objections against elections by districts. 1. It is impracticable; the people cannot be brought to one place for the purpose; and whether brought to the same place or not, numberless frauds would be unavoidable. 2. Small States forming part of the same district with a large one, or large part of a large one, would have no chance of gaining an appointment for its citizens of merit. 3. A new source of discord would be opened between different parts of the same district.

Mr. Pinckney thought the second branch ought to be permanent and independent, and that the members of it would be rendered more so by receiving their appointment from the State Legislatures. This mode would avoid the [rivalries] and discontents incident to the election by districts. He was for dividing the States into three classes according to their respective sizes, and for allowing to the first class three members—to the second two, and to the third one.

Debate on Veto of State Laws (June 8)

The Convention soon faced directly the most debilitating weakness of the Articles of Confederation: the inability of Congress to control state legislation that violated national laws or treaties. Strong sentiment existed, as the Virginia Plan revealed, for explicit power in Congress to invalidate, or "negative" "improper" state laws. (At the conclusion of the debate, the motion for a Congressional negative on state laws was defeated, 7 states no, 3 states yes, and 1 state divided.)

MR. PINCKNEY moved "that the National Legislature should have authority to negative all laws which they should judge to be improper." He urged that such a universality of the power was indispensably necessary to render it effectual; that the States must be kept in due subordination to the nation; that if the States were left to act of themselves in any case, it would be impossible to defend the national prerogatives, however extensive they might be on paper; that the acts of Congress had been defeated by this means; nor had foreign treaties escaped repeated violations; that this universal negative was in fact the corner stone of an efficient national government; that under the British government the negative of the Crown had been found beneficial, and the *States* are more one nation now, than the *Colonies* were then.

MR. MADISON seconded the motion. He could not but regard an indefinite power to negative legislative acts of the States as absolutely necessary to a perfect system. Experience had evinced a constant tendency in the States to encroach on the federal authority; to violate national Treaties; to infringe the rights and interests of each other; to oppress the weaker party within their respective jurisdictions. A negative was the mildest expedient that could be devised for preventing these mischiefs. The existence of such a check would prevent attempts to commit them. Should no such precaution be engrafted, the only remedy would lie in an appeal to coercion. Was such a remedy eligible? was it practicable? Could the national resources, if exerted to the utmost enforce a national decree against Massachusetts abetted perhaps by several of her neighbours? It would not be possible. A small proportion of the Community, in a compact situation, acting on the defensive, and at one of its extremities might at any time bid defiance to the National authority. Any government for the United States formed on the supposed practicability of using force against the unconstitutional proceedings of the States, would prove as visionary and fallacious as the government of Congress. The negative would render the use of force unnecessary. The States could of themselves then pass no operative act, any more than one branch of a Legislature where there are two branches, can proceed without the other. But in order to give the negative this efficacy, it must extend to all cases. A discrimination would only be a fresh source of contention between the two authorities. In a word, to recur to the illustrations borrowed from the planetary system. This prerogative of the General government is the great pervading principle that must control the centrifugal tendency of the States; which, without it, will continually fly out of their proper orbits and destroy the order and harmony of the political System.

MR. WILLIAMSON was against giving a power that might restrain the States from regulating their internal police.

MR. GERRY could not see the extent of such a power, and was against every power that was not necessary. He thought a remonstrance against unreasonable acts of the States would reclaim them. If it should not force might be resorted to. He had no objection to authorize a negative to paper money and similar measures. When the confederation was depending before Congress, Massachusetts was then for inserting the power of emitting paper money among the exclusive powers of Congress. He observed that the proposed negative would extend to the regulations of the Militia, a matter on which the existence of a State might depend. The National Legislature with such a power may enslave the States. Such an idea as this will never be acceded to. It has never been suggested or conceived among the people. No speculative projector, and there are enough of that character among us, in politics as well as in other things, has in any pamphlet or newspaper thrown out the idea. The States too have different interests and are ignorant of each other's interests. The negative therefore will be abused. New States too having separate views from the old States will never come into the Union. They may even be under some foreign influence; are they in such case to participate in the negative on the will of the other States?

MR. SHERMAN thought the cases in which the negative ought to be exercised, might be defined. He wished the point might not be decided till a trial at least should be made for that purpose.

MR. WILSON would not say what modifications of the proposed power might be practicable or expedient. But however novel it might appear the principle of it when viewed with a close and steady eye, is right. There is no instance in which the laws say that the individual should be bound in one case, and at liberty to judge whether he will obey or disobey in another. The cases are parallel. Abuses of the power over the individual person may happen as well as over the individual States. Federal liberty is to States, what civil liberty, is to private individuals. And States are not more unwilling to purchase it, by the necessary concession of their political sovereignty, than the savage is to purchase civil liberty by the surrender of his personal sovereignty, which he enjoys in a State of nature. A definition of the cases in which the Negative should be exercised, is impracticable. A discretion must be left on one side or the other? will it not be most safely lodged on the side of the National government? Among the first sentiments expressed in the first Congress one was that Virginia is no more, that Massachusetts is no, that Pennsylvania is no more etc., *etc.* We are now one nation of brethren. We must bury all local interests and distinctions. This language continued for some time. The tables at length began to turn. No sooner were the State governments formed than their jealousy and ambition began to display themselves. Each endeavoured to cut a slice from the common loaf, to add to its own morsel, till at length the confederation became frittered down to the impotent condition in which it now stands. Review the progress of the articles of Confederation through Congress and compare the first and last draught of it. To correct its vices is the business of this convention. One of its vices is the want of an effectual control in the whole over its parts. What danger is there that the whole will unnecessarily sacrifice a part? But reverse the case, and leave the whole at the mercy of each part, and will not the general interest be continually sacrificed to local interests?

 Mr. Dickinson deemed it impossible to draw a line between the cases proper and improper for the exercise of the negative. We must take our choice of two things. We must either subject the States to the danger of being injured by the power of the National government or the latter to the danger of being injured by that of the States. He thought the danger greater from the States. To leave the power doubtful, would be opening another spring of discord, and he was for shutting as many of them as possible.

 Mr. Bedford. In answer to his colleague's question where would be the danger to the States from this power, would refer him to the smallness of his own State which may be injured at pleasure without redress. It was meant he found to strip the small States of their equal right of suffrage. In this case Delaware would have about one ninetieth for its share in the General Councils, whilst Pennsylvania and Virginia would possess one third of the whole. Is there no difference of interests, no rival-ship of commerce, of manufactures? Will not these large States crush the small ones whenever they stand in the way of their ambitious or interested views. This shows the impossibility of adopting such a system as that on the table, or any other founded on a change in the principle of representation. And after all, if a State does not obey the law of the new System, must not force be resorted to as the only ultimate remedy, in this as in any other system. It seems as if Pennsylvania and Virginia by the conduct of their deputies wished to provide a system in which they would have an enormous and monstrous influence. Besides, how can it be thought that the proposed negative can be exercised? are the laws of the States to be suspended in the most urgent cases until they can be sent seven or eight hundred miles, and undergo the deliberations of a body who may be incapable of Judging of them? Is the National Legislature too to sit continually in order to revise the laws of the States?

MR. MADISON observed that the difficulties which had been stated were worthy of attention and ought to be answered before the question was put. The case of laws of urgent necessity must be provided for by some emanation of the power from the National government into each State so far as to give a temporary assent at least. This was the practice in Royal Colonies before the Revolution and would not have been inconvenient, if the supreme power of negativing had been faithful to the American interest, and had possessed the necessary information. He supposed that the negative might be very properly lodged in the senate alone, and that the more numerous and expensive branch therefore might not be obliged to sit constantly.—He asked Mr. Bedford what would be the consequence to the small States of a dissolution of the Union which seemed likely to happen if no effectual substitute was made for the defective System existing, and he did not conceive any effectual system could be substituted on any other basis than that of a proportional suffrage? If the large States possessed the avarice and ambition with which they were charged, would the small ones in their neighbourhood, be more secure when all control of a General Government was withdrawn.

MR. BUTLER was vehement against the Negative in the proposed extent, as cutting off all hope of equal justice to the distant States. The people there would not he was sure give it a hearing.

The New Jersey Plan (June 15)

After three days of increasingly contentious debate and votes on many detailed points, the Convention reported a series of resolves that represented its decisions thus far. Most of the major points of the Virginia Plan had been accepted, but delegates who opposed such marked strengthening of the national government, and especially those from small states who wanted to retain the equal voting power of the states, sought to put forward a plan more to their liking. After a day's adjournment to settle on such a plan, William Paterson of New Jersey offered a series of resolutions embodying the more "purely federal" plan; that is, one maintaining the "league of states" form of the Articles of Confederation.

    1. Resolved that the articles of Confederation ought to be so revised, corrected and enlarged, as to render the federal Constitution adequate to the exigencies of Government, and the preservation of the Union.

    2. Resolved that in addition to the powers vested in the United States in Congress, by the present existing articles of Confederation, they be authorized to pass acts for raising a revenue, by levying a duty or duties on all goods or merchandizes of foreign growth or manufacture, imported into any part of the United States, by Stamps on paper, vellum or parchment, and by a postage on all letters or packages passing through the general post-office, to be applied to such federal purposes as they shall deem proper and expedient; to make rules and regulations for the collection thereof; and the same from time to time, to alter and amend in such manner as they shall think proper: to pass Acts for the regulation of trade and commerce as well with foreign nations as with each other: provided that all punishments, fines, forfeitures and penalties to be incurred for contravening such acts rules and regulations shall be adjudged by the Common law Judiciaries of the State in which any offence contrary to the true intent and meaning of such Acts rules and regulations shall have been committed or perpetrated, with liberty of commencing in the first instance all suits and prosecutions for that purpose in the superior common law Judiciary in such State, subject nevertheless, for the correction of all errors, both in law and fact in rendering Judgment, to an appeal to the Judiciary of the United States.

    3. Resolved that whenever requisitions shall be necessary, instead of the rule for making requisitions mentioned in the articles of Confederation, the United

States in Congress be authorized to make such requisitions in proportion to the whole number of white and other free citizens and inhabitants of every age sex and condition including those bound to servitude for a term of years and three fifths of all other persons not comprehended in the foregoing description, except Indians not paying taxes; that if such requisitions be not complied with, in the time specified therein, to direct the collection thereof in the non complying States and for that purpose to devise and pass acts directing and authorizing the same; provided that none of the powers hereby vested in the United States in Congress shall be exercised without the consent of at least States, and in that proportion if the number of Confederated States should hereafter be increased or diminished.

4. Resolved that the United States in Congress be authorized to elect a federal Executive to consist of persons, to continue in office for the term of years, to receive punctually at stated times a fixed compensation for their services, in which no increase or diminution shall be made so as to affect the persons composing the Executive at the time of such increase or diminution, to be paid out of the federal treasury; to be incapable of holding any other office or appointment during their time of service and for years thereafter; to be ineligible a second time, and removeable by Congress on application by a majority of the Executives of the several States; that the Executives besides their general authority to execute the federal acts ought to appoint all federal officers not otherwise provided for, and to direct all military operations; provided that none of the persons composing the federal Executive shall on any occasion take command of any troops, so as personally to conduct any enterprise as General or in other capacity.

5. Resolved that a federal Judiciary be established to consist of a supreme Tribunal the Judges of which to be appointed by the Executive, and to hold their offices during good behaviour, to receive punctually at stated times a fixed compensation for their services in which no increase or diminution shall be made, so as to affect the persons actually in office at the time of such increase or diminution; that the Judiciary so established shall have authority to hear and determine in the first instance on all impeachments of federal officers, and by way of appeal in the [last] resort in all cases touching the rights of Ambassadors, in all cases of captures from an enemy, in all cases of piracies and felonies on the high Seas, in all cases in which foreigners may be interested, in the construction of any treaty or treaties, or which may arise on any of the Acts for regulation of trade, or the collection of the federal Revenue: that none of the Judiciary shall during the time they remain in office be capable of receiving or holding any other office or appointment during their time of service, or for

thereafter.

6. Resolved that all Acts of the United States in Congress made by virtue and in pursuance of the powers hereby and by the articles of Confederation vested in them, and all Treaties made and ratified under the authority of the United States shall be the supreme law of the respective States so far forth as those Acts or Treaties shall relate to the said States or their Citizens, and that the Judiciary of the several States shall be bound thereby in their decisions, any thing in the respective laws of the Individual States to the contrary notwithstanding; and that if any State, or any body of men in any State shall oppose or prevent the carrying into execution such acts or treaties, the federal Executive shall be authorized to call forth the power of the Confederated States, or so much thereof as may be necessary to enforce and compel an obedience to such Acts, or an observance of such Treaties.

7. Resolved that provision be made for the admission of new States into the Union.

8. Resolved the rule for naturalization ought to be the same in every State.

9. Resolved that a Citizen of one State committing an offence in another State of the Union, shall be deemed guilty of the same offence as if it had been committed by a Citizen of the State in which the offence was committed.

Debate of the New Jersey Plan (June 16)

The next day Paterson spoke in defense of the New Jersey Plan, while James Wilson and Edmund Randolph explained why they still preferred the Virginia Plan.

MR. PATERSON said as he had on former occasion given his sentiments on the plan proposed by Mr. Randolph he would now avoiding repetition as much as possible give his reasons in favor of that proposed by himself. He preferred it because it accorded 1. with the powers of the Convention, 2. with the sentiments of the people. If the confederacy was radically wrong, let us return to our States, and obtain larger powers, not assume them of ourselves. I came here not to speak my own sentiments, but the sentiments of those who sent me. Our object is not such a government as may be best in itself, but such a one as our Constituents have authorized us to prepare, and as they will approve. If we argue the matter on the supposition that no Confederacy at present exists, it can not be denied that all the States stand on the footing of equal sovereignty. All therefore must concur before any can be bound. If a proportional representation be right, why do we not vote so here? If we argue on the fact that a federal compact actually exists, and consult the articles of it we still find an equal Sovereignty to be the basis of it. He reads the fifth article of Confederation giving each State a vote—and the thirteenth declaring that no alteration shall be made without unanimous consent. This is the nature of all treaties. What is unanimously done, must be unanimously undone. It was observed [by Mr. Wilson] that the larger States gave up the point, not because it was right, but because the circumstances of the moment urged the concession. Be it so. Are they for that reason at liberty to take it back. Can the donor resume his gift without the consent of the donee. This doctrine may be convenient, but it is a doctrine that will sacrifice the lesser States. The large States acceded readily to the confederacy. It was the small ones that came in reluctantly and slowly. N. Jersey and Maryland were the two last, the former objecting to the want of power in Congress over trade: both of them to the want of power to appropriate the vacant territory to the benefit of the whole.—If the sovereignty of the States is to be maintained, the Representatives must be drawn immediately from the States, not from the people: and we have no power to vary the idea of equal sovereignty. The only expedient that will cure the difficulty, is that of throwing the States into Hotchpot. To say that this is impracticable, will not make it so. Let it be tried, and we shall see whether the Citizens of Massachusetts, Pennsylvania and Virginia accede to it. It will be objected that Coercion will be impracticable. But will it be more so in one plan than the other? Its efficacy will depend on the quantum of power collected, not on its being drawn from the States, or from the individuals; and according to his plan it may be exerted on individuals as well as according that of Mr. Randolph. A distinct executive and Judiciary also were equally provided by his plan. It is urged that two branches in the Legislature are necessary. Why? for the purpose of a check. But the reason of the precaution is not applicable to this case. Within a particular State, where party heats prevail, such a check may be necessary. In such a body as Congress it is less necessary, and besides, the delegations of the different States are checks on each other. Do the people at large complain of Congress? No, what they wish is that Congress may have more power. If the power now proposed be not enough, the people hereafter will make additions to it. With proper powers Congress will act with more energy and wisdom than the proposed National Legislature; being fewer in number, and more secreted and refined by the mode of election. The plan of Mr. Randolph will also be enormously expensive. Allowing Georgia and Delaware two representatives each in the popular branch the aggregate number of that branch will be 180. Add to it half as many for the other branch and you have 270. Members coming once at least a year from the most distant as well as the most central parts of the republic. In the present deranged state of our finances can so expensive a system be seriously thought of? By enlarging the powers of Congress the greatest part of this expense will be saved, and all purposes will be answered. At least a trial ought to be made.

MR. WILSON entered into a contrast of the principal points of the two plans so far he said as there had been time to examine the one last proposed. These points were 1. in the Virginia plan there are two and in some degree three branches in the Legislature: in the plan from N. J. there is to be a *single* legislature only—2. Representation of the people at large is the basis of the one:—the State Legislatures, the pillars of the other—3. Proportional representation prevails in one:—equality of suffrage in the other—4. A single Executive Magistrate is at the head of the one—a plurality is held out in the other.—5. In the one the majority of the people of the United States must prevail:—in the other a minority may prevail. 6. The National Legislature is to make laws in all cases to which the separate States are incompetent and—in place of this Congress are to have additional power in a few cases only—7. A negative on the laws of the States:—in place of this coercion to be substituted—8. The Executive to be removeable on impeachment and conviction;—in one plan: in the other to be removeable at the instance of majority of the Executives of the States—9. Revision of the laws provided for in one—no such check in the other—10. Inferior national tribunals in one—none such in the other. 11. In the one, jurisdiction of National tribunals to extend etc., etc.—; an appellate jurisdiction only allowed in the other. 12. Here the jurisdiction is to extend to all cases affecting the National peace and harmony: there, a few cases only are marked out. 13. Finally the ratification is in this to be by the people themselves:—in that by the legislative authorities according to the thirteenth article of Confederation.

With regard to the *power of the Convention,* he conceived himself authorized to *conclude nothing,* but to be at liberty to *propose any thing.* In this particular he felt himself perfectly indifferent to the two plans.

With regard to the *sentiments of the people,* he conceived it difficult to know precisely what they are. Those of the particular circle in which one moved, were commonly mistaken for the general voice. He could not persuade himself that the State Governments and Sovereignties were so much the idols of the people, nor a National Government so obnoxious to them, as some supposed. Why should a National Government be unpopular? Has it less dignity? Will each Citizen enjoy under it less liberty or protection? Will a Citizen of *Delaware* be degraded by becoming a Citizen of the *United States?* Where do the people look at present for relief from the evils of which they complain? Is it from an internal reform of their Governments? No, Sir. It is from the National Councils that relief is expected. For these reasons he did not fear, that the people would not follow us into a national Government and it will be a further recommendation of Mr. Randolph's plan that it is to be submitted to *them,* and not to the *Legislatures,* for ratification.

Proceeding now to the first point on which he had contrasted the two plans, he observed that anxious as he was for some augmentation of the federal powers, it would be with extreme reluctance indeed that he could ever consent to give powers to Congress; he had two reasons either of which was sufficient. 1. Congress, as a Legislative body does not stand on the people. 2. It is a *single* body. He would not repeat the remarks he had formerly made on the principles of Representation. He would only say that an inequality in it, has ever been a poison contaminating every branch of Government. In Great Britain where this poison has had a full operation, the security of private rights is owing entirely to the purity of Her tribunals of Justice, the Judges of which are neither appointed nor paid, by a venal Parliament. The political liberty of that Nation, owing to the inequality of representation is at the mercy of its rulers. He means not to insinuate that there is any parallel between the situation of that Country and ours at present. But it is a lesson we ought not to disregard, that the smallest bodies in

Great Britain are notoriously the most corrupt. Every other source of influence must also be stronger in small than large bodies of men. When Lord Chesterfield had told us that one of the Dutch provinces had been seduced into the views of France, he need not have added, that it was not Holland, but one of the *smallest* of them. There are facts among ourselves which are known to all. Passing over others, he will only remark that the *Impost*, so anxiously wished for by the public was defeated not by any of the *larger* States in the Union. 2. *Congress is a single Legislature.* Despotism comes on Mankind in different Shapes, sometimes in an Executive, sometimes in a Military, one. Is there no danger of a Legislative despotism? Theory and practice both proclaim it. If the Legislative authority be not restrained, there can be neither liberty nor stability; and it can only be restrained by dividing it within itself, into distinct and independent branches. In a single House there is no check, but the inadequate one, of the virtue and good sense of those who compose it.

On another great point, the contrast was equally favorable to the plan reported by the Committee of the whole. It vested the Executive powers in a single Magistrate. The plan of New Jersey, vested them in a plurality. In order to control the Legislative authority, you must divide it. In order to control the Executive you must unite it. One man will be more responsible than three. Three will contend among themselves till one becomes the master of his colleagues. In the triumvirates of Rome first Caesar, then Augustus, are witnesses of this truth. The Kings of Sparta, and the Consuls of Rome prove also the factious consequences of dividing the Executive Magistracy. Having already taken up so much time he would not he said proceed to any of the other points. Those on which he had dwelt, are sufficient of themselves: and on a decision of them, the fate of the others will depend....

Mr. Randolph was not scrupulous on the point of power. When the salvation of the Republic was at stake, it would be treason to our trust, not to propose what we found necessary. He painted in strong colours, the imbecility of the existing Confederacy, and the danger of delaying a substantial reform. In answer to the objection drawn from the sense of our Constituents as denoted by their acts relating to the Convention and the objects of their deliberation, he observed that as each State acted separately in the case, it would have been indecent for it to have charged the existing Constitution with all the vices which it might have perceived in it. The first State that set on foot this experiment would not have been justified in going so far, ignorant as it was of the opinion of others, and sensible as it must have been of the uncertainty of a successful issue to the experiment. There are certainly seasons of a peculiar nature where the ordinary cautions must be dispensed with; and this is certainly one of them. He would not as far as depended on him leave any thing that seemed necessary, undone. The present moment is favorable, and is probably the last that will offer.

The true question is whether we shall adhere to the federal plan, or introduce the national plan. The insufficiency of the former has been fully displayed by the trial already made. There are but two modes, by which the end of a General Government can be attained: the first is by coercion as proposed by Mister Paterson's plan. 2. By real legislation as proposed by the other plan. Coercion he pronounced to be *impracticable, expensive, cruel to individuals.* It tended also to habituate the instruments of it to shed the blood and riot in the spoils of their fellow Citizens, and consequently trained them up for the service of ambition. We must resort therefore to a National *Legislation over individuals,* for which Congress are unfit. To vest such power in them, would be blending the Legislative with the Executive, contrary to the recorded maxim on this subject: If the Union of these powers heretofore in Congress has been safe, it has been owing to the general impotency of that body. Congress are moreover not elected by the people, but by the Legislatures who retain even a power of recall. They have therefore no will of their own, they are a mere diplomatic body, and are always obsequious to the views of the States, who are always encroaching on the authority of the United States. A provision for harmony among the States, as in trade, naturalization, etc.—for crushing rebellion whenever it may rear its crest—and for certain other general benefits, must be made. The powers for these purposes, can never be given to a body, inadequate as Congress are in point of representation, elected in the mode in which they are, and possessing no more confidence than they do: for notwithstanding what has been said to the contrary, his own experience satisfied him that a rooted distrust of Congress pretty generally prevailed. A National Government alone, properly constituted, will answer the purpose; and he begged it to be considered that the present is the last moment for establishing one. After this select experiment, the people will yield to despair.

Plan for National Government (June 18)

Sensing that the Convention had been sent into disarray by the dissension over the Virginia and New Jersey Plans, and thus might be open to a radically different form of government, Alexander Hamilton made a long speech presenting a plan vastly strengthening the national government.

MR. HAMILTON had been hitherto silent on the business before the Convention, partly from respect to others whose superior abilities age and experience rendered him unwilling to bring forward ideas dissimilar to theirs, and partly from his delicate situation with respect to his own State, to whose sentiments as expressed by his Colleagues, he could by no means accede. The crisis however which now marked our affairs, was too serious to permit any scruples whatever to prevail over the duty imposed on every man to contribute his efforts for the public safety and happiness. He was obliged therefore to declare himself unfriendly to both plans. He was particularly opposed to that from New Jersey, being fully convinced, that no amendment of the Confederation, leaving the States in possession of their Sovereignty could possibly answer the purpose. On the other hand he confessed he was much discouraged by the amazing extent of the Country in expecting the desired blessings from any general sovereignty that could be substituted.—As to the powers of the Convention, he thought the doubts started on that subject had arisen from distinctions and reasonings too subtle. A *federal* Government he conceived to mean an association of independent Communities into one. Different Confederacies have different powers, and exercise them in different ways. In some instances the powers are exercised over collective bodies; in others over individuals, as in the German Diet—and among ourselves in cases of piracy. Great latitude therefore must be given to the signification of the term. The plan last proposed departs itself from the *federal* idea, as understood by some, since it is to operate eventually on individuals. He agreed moreover with the Honorable gentleman from Virginia [Mr. Randolph] that we owed it to our Country, to do on this emergency whatever we should deem essential to its happiness. The States sent us here to provide for the exigences of the Union. To rely on and propose any plan not adequate to these exigences, merely because it was not clearly within our powers, would be to sacrifice the means to the end. It may be said that the *States* can not *ratify* a plan not within the purview of the article of Confederation providing for alterations and amendments. But may not the States themselves in which no constitutional authority equal to this purpose exists in the Legislatures, have had in view a reference to the people at large. In the Senate of New York, a proviso was moved, that no act of the Convention should be binding untill it should be referred to the people and ratified; and the motion was lost by a single voice only, the reason assigned against it being, that it might possibly be found an inconvenient shackle.

The great question is what provision shall we make for the happiness of our Country? He would first make a comparative examination of the two plans—prove that there were essential defects in both—and point out such changes as might render a *national one*, efficacious.—The great and essential principles necessary for the support of Government are 1. An active and constant interest in supporting it. This principle does not exist in the States in favor of the federal Government. They have evidently in a high degree, the esprit de corps. They constantly pursue internal interests adverse to those of the whole. They have their particular debts—their particular plans of finance *etc*. All these when opposed to, invariably prevail over the requisitions and plans of Congress. 2. The love of power. Men love power. The same remarks are applicable to this principle. The States have constantly shown a disposition rather to regain the powers delegated by them than to part with more, or to give effect to what they had parted with. The ambition of their demagogues is known to hate the control of the General Government. It may be remarked too that the Citizens have not that anxiety to prevent a dissolution of the General Government as of the particular Governments. A dissolution of the latter would be fatal; of the former would still leave the purposes of Government attainable to a considerable degree. Consider what such a State as Virginia will be in a few years, a few compared with the life of nations. How strongly will it feel its importance and self-sufficiency? 3. An habitual attachment of the people. The whole force of this tie is on the side of the State Government. Its sovereignty is immediately before the eyes of the people: its protection is immediately enjoyed by them. From its hand distributive justice, and all those acts which familiarize and endear Government to a people, are dispensed to them. 4. *Force* by which may be understood a *coertion of laws* or *coertion of arms*. Congress have not the former except in few cases. In particular States, this coercion is nearly sufficient; though he held it in most cases, not entirely so. A certain portion of military force is absolutely necessary in large communities. Massachusetts is now feeling this necessity and making provision for it. But how can this force be exerted on the States collectively. It is impossible. It amounts to a war between the parties. Foreign powers also will not be idle spectators. They will interpose, the confusion will increase, and a dissolution of the Union ensue. 5. *Influence*. He did not mean corruption, but a dispensation of those regular honors and emoluments, which produce an attachment to the Government. Almost all the weight of these is on the side of the States; and must continue so as long as the States continue to exist. All the passions then we see, of avarice, ambition, interest, which govern most individuals, and all public bodies, fall into the current of the States, and do not flow in the stream of the General Government. The former therefore will generally be an overmatch for the General Government and render any confederacy, in its very nature precarious. Theory is in this case fully confirmed by experience. The Amphyctionic Council had it would seem ample powers for general purposes. It had in particular the power of fining and using force against delinquent members. What was the consequence. Their decrees were mere signals of war. The Phocian war is a striking example of it. Philip at length taking advantage of their disunion, and insinuating himself into their Councils, made himself master of their fortunes. The German Confederacy affords another lesson. The authority of Charlemagne seemed to be as great as could be necessary. The great feudal chiefs however, exercising their local sovereignties, soon felt the spirit and found the means of, encroachments, which reduced the imperial authority to a nominal sovereignty. The Diet has succeeded, which though aided by a Prince at its head, of great authority independently of his imperial attributes, is a striking illustration of the weakness of Confederated Governments. Other examples instruct us in the same truth. The Swiss cantons have scarce any Union at all, and have been more than once at war with one another.—How then are all these evils to be avoided? Only by such a compleat sovereignty in the general Government as will turn all the strong principles and passions above mentioned on its side. Does the scheme of New Jersey produce this effect? Does it afford any substantial remedy whatever? On the contrary it labors under great defects, and the defect of some of its provisions will destroy the efficacy of others. It gives a direct revenue to Congress but this will not be sufficient. The balance can only be supplied by requisitions: which experience proves can not be relied on. If States are to deliberate on the mode, they will also deliberate on the object of the supplies, and will grant or not grant as they approve or disapprove of it. The delinquency of one will invite and countenance it in others. Quotas too must in the nature of things be so unequal as to produce the same evil. To what standard will you resort? Land is a fallacious one. Compare Holland with Russia: France or England with other countries of Europe. Pennsylvania with North Carolina. Will the relative pecuniary abilities in those instances, correspond with the relative value of land? Take numbers of inhabitants for the rule and make like comparison of different countries, and you will find it to be equally unjust. The different degrees of industry and improvement in different Countries render the first object a precarious measure of wealth. Much depends too on *situation.* Connecticut, New Jersey and North Carolina, not being commercial States and contributing to the wealth of the commercial ones, can never bear quotas assessed by the ordinary rules of proportion. They will and must fail in their duty, their example will be followed, and the Union itself be dissolved. Whence then is the national revenue to be drawn? from Commerce? even from exports which notwithstanding the common opinion are fit objects of moderate taxation, from excise, etc, *etc.* These though not equal, are less unequal than quotas. Another destructive ingredient in the plan, is that equality of suffrage which is so much desired by the small States. It is not in human nature that Virginia and the large States should consent to it, or if they did that they should long abide by it. It shocks too much the ideas of Justice, and every human feeling. Bad principles in a Government though slow are sure in their operation, and will gradually destroy it. A doubt has been raised whether Congress at present have a right to keep Ships or troops in time of peace. He leans to the negative. Mr. Paterson's plan provides no remedy.—If the powers proposed were adequate, the organization of Congess is such that they could never be properly and effectually exercised. The members of Congress being chosen by the States and subject to recall, represent all the local prejudices. Should the powers be found effectual, they will from time to time be heaped on them, till a tyrannic sway shall be established. The general power whatever be its form if it preserves itself, must swallow up the State powers. Otherwise it will be swallowed up by them. It is against all the principles of a good Government to vest the requisite powers in such a body as Congress. Two Sovereignties can not co-exist within the same limits. Giving powers to Congress must eventuate in a bad Government or in no Government. The plan of New Jersey therefore will not do. What then is to be done? Here he was embarrassed. The extent of the Country to be governed, discouraged him. The expense of a general Government was also formidable; unless there were a diminution of expense on the side of the State Government as the case would admit. If they were extinguished, he was persuaded that great economy might be obtained by substituting a general Government. He did not mean however to shock the public opinion by proposing such a measure. On the other hand he saw no *other* necessity for declining it. They are not necessary for any of the great purposes of commerce, revenue, or agriculture. Subordinate authorities he was aware would be necessary. There must be district tribunals: corporations for local purposes. But cui bono, the vast and expensive apparatus now appertaining to the States. The only difficulty of a serious nature which occurred to him, was that of drawing representatives from the extremes to the center of the Community. What inducements can be offered that will suffice? The moderate wages for the first branch would only be a bait to little demagogues. Three dollars or thereabouts he supposed would be the utmost. The Senate he feared from a similar cause, would be filled by certain undertakers who wish for particular offices under the Government. This view of the subject almost led him to despair that a Republican Government could be established over so great an extent. He was sensible at the same time that it would be unwise to propose one of any other form. In his private opinion he had no scruple in declaring, supported as he was by the opinions of so many of the wise and good, that the British Government was the best in the world: and that he doubted much whether any thing short of it would do in America. He hoped Gentlemen of different opinions would bear with him in this, and begged them to recollect the change of opinion on this subject which had taken place and was still going on. It was once thought that the power of Congress was amply sufficient to secure the end of their institution. The error was now seen by every one. The members most tenacious of republicanism, he observed, were as loud as any in declaiming against the vices of democracy. This progress of the public mind led him to anticipate the time, when others as well as himself would join in the praise bestowed by Mr. Neckar on the British Constitution, namely, that it is the only Government in the world "which unites public strength with individual security."—In every community where industry is encouraged, there will be a division of it into the few and the many. Hence separate interests will arise. There will be debtors and creditors *etc*. Give all power to the many, they will oppress the few. Both therefore ought to have power, that each may defend itself against the other. To the want of this check we owe our paper money, instalment laws *etc*. To the proper adjustment of it the British owe the excellence of their Constitution. Their house of Lords is a most noble institution. Having nothing to hope for by a change, and a sufficient interest by means of their property, in being faithful to the interest, they form a permanent barrier against every pernicious innovation, whether attempted on the part of the Crown or of the Commons. No temporary Senate will have firmness enough to answer the purpose. The Senate [of Maryland] which seems to be so much appealed to, has not yet been sufficiently tried. Had the people been unanimous and eager, in the late appeal to them on the subject of a paper emission they would have yielded to the torrent. Their acquiescing in such an appeal is a proof of it.—Gentlemen differ in their opinions concerning the necessary checks, from the different estimates they form of the human passions. They suppose seven years a sufficient period to give the senate an adequate firmness, from not duly considering the amazing violence and turbulence of the democratic spirit. When a great object of Government is pursued, which seizes the popular passions, they spread like wild fire, and become irresistable. He appealed to the gentlemen from the New England States whether experience had not there verified the remark.—As to the Executive, it seemed to be admitted that no good could be established on Republican principles. Was not this giving up the merits of the question: for can there be a good Government without a good Executive. The English model was the only good one on this subject. The Hereditary interest of the King was so interwoven with that of the Nation, and his personal emoluments so great, that he was placed above the danger of being corrupted from abroad—and at the same time was both sufficiently independent and sufficiently controled, to answer the purpose of the institution at home. One of the weak sides of Republics was their being liable to foreign influence and corruption. Men of little character, acquiring great power become easily the tools of intermedling Neighbors. Sweden was a striking instance. The French and English had each their parties during the late Revolution which was affected by the predominant influence of the former.—What is the inference from all these observations? That we ought to go as far in order to attain stability and permanency, as republican principles will admit. Let one branch of the Legislature hold their places for life or at least during good behaviour. Let the Executive also be for life. He appealed to the feelings of the members present whether a term of seven years, would induce the sacrifices of private affairs which an acceptance of public trust would require, so as to ensure the services of the best Citizens. On this plan we should have in the Senate a permanent will, a weighty interest, which would answer essential purposes. But is this a Republican Government, it will be asked? Yes if all the magistrates are appointed, and vacancies are filled, by the people, or a process of election originating with the people. He was sensible that an Executive constituted as he proposed would have in fact but little of the power and independence that might be necessary. On the other plan of appointing him for 7 years, he thought the Executive ought to have but little power. He would be ambitious, with the means of making creatures; and as the object of his ambition would be to *prolong* his power, it is probable that in case of a war, he would avail himself of the emergence, to evade or refuse a degradation from his place. An Executive for life has not this motive for forgetting his fidelity, and will therefore be a safer depository of power. It will be objected probably, that such an Executive will be an *elective Monarch*, and will give birth to the tumults which characterize that form of Government. He would reply that *Monarch* is an indefinite term. It marks not either the degree or duration of power. If this Executive Magistrate would be a monarch for life—the other proposed by the Report from the Committee of the whole, would be a monarch for seven years. The circumstance of being elective was also applicable to both. It had been observed by judicious writers that elective monarchies would be the best if they could be guarded against the *tumults* excited by the ambition and intrigues of competitors. He was not sure that tumults were an inseparable evil. He rather thought this character of Elective Monarchies had been taken rather from particular cases than from general principles. The election of Roman Emperors was made by the *Army*. In *Poland* the election is made by great rival *princes* with independent power, and ample means, of raising commotions. In the German Empire, the appointment is made by the Electors and Princes, who have equal motives and means, for exciting cabals and parties. Might not such a mode of election be devised among ourselves as will defend the community against these effects in any dangerous degree? Having made these observations he would read to the Committee a sketch of a plan which he should prefer to either of those under consideration. He was aware that it went beyond the ideas of most members. But will such a plan be adopted out of doors? In return he would ask will the people adopt the other plan? At present they will adopt neither. But he sees the Union dissolving or already dissolved—he sees evils operating in the States which must soon cure the people of their fondness for democracies—he sees that a great progress has been already made and is still going on in the public mind. He thinks therefore that the people will in time be unshackled from their prejudices; and whenever that happens, they will themselves not be satisfied at stopping where the plan of Mr. Randolph would place them, but be ready to go as far at least as he proposes. He did not mean to offer the paper he had sketched as a proposition to the Committee. It was meant only to give a more correct view of his ideas, and to suggest the amendments which he should probably propose to the plan of Mr. Randolph in the proper stages of its future discussion. He read his sketch, in the words following, to wit:

"I. The Supreme Legislative power of the United States of America to be vested in two different bodies of men; the one to be called the Assembly, the other the Senate who together shall form the Legislature of the United States with power to pass all laws whatsoever subject to the Negative hereafter mentioned.

II. The Assembly to consist of persons elected by the people to serve for three years.

III. The Senate to consist of persons elected to serve during good behaviour; their election to be made by electors chosen for that purpose by the people: in order to do this the States to be divided into election districts. On the death, removal or resignation of any Senator his place to be filled out of the district from which he came.

IV. The supreme Executive authority of the United States to be vested in a Governor to be elected to serve during good behaviour—the election to be made by Electors chosen by the people in the Election Districts aforesaid.—The authorities and functions of the Executive to be as follows: to have a negative on all laws about to be passed, and the execution of all laws passed; to have the direction of war when authorized or begun; to have with the advice and approbation of the Senate the power of making all treaties; to have the sole appointment of the heads or chief officers of the departments of Finance, War and Foreign Affairs; to have the nomination of all other officers (Ambassadors to foreign Nations included) subject to the approbation or rejection of the Senate; to have the power of pardoning all offences except Treason; which he shall not pardon without the approbation of the Senate.

V. On the death, resignation or removal of the Governor his authorities to be exercised by the President of the Senate till a Successor be appointed.

VI. The Senate to have the sole power of declaring war, the power of advising and approving all Treaties, the power of approving or rejecting all appointments of officers except the heads or chiefs of the departments of Finance, War and Foreign Affairs.

VII. The supreme Judicial authority to be vested in Judges to hold their offices during good behaviour with adequate and permanent salaries. This Court to have original jurisdiction in all causes of capture, and an appelative jurisdiction in all causes in which the revenues of the general Government or the Citizens of foreign Nations are concerned.

VIII. The Legislature of the United States to have power to institute Courts in each State for the determination of all matters of general concern.

IX. The Governor Senators and all officers of the United States to be liable to impeachment for mal-and corrupt conduct; and upon conviction to be removed from office, and disqualified for holding any place of trust or profit.—All impeachments to be tried by a Court to consist of the Chief [Justice] or Judge of the superior Court of Law of each State, provided such Judge shall hold his place during good behavior, and have a permanent salary.

X. All laws of the particular States contrary to the Constitution or laws of the United States to be utterly void; and the better to prevent such laws being passed, the Governor or president of each State shall be appointed by the General Government and shall have a negative upon the laws about to be passed in the State of which he is Governor or President.

XI. No State to have any forces land or Naval; and the Militia of all the States to be under the sole and exclusive direction of the United States, the officers of which to be appointed and commissioned by them."

Opposition to the New Jersey Plan (June 19)

The next day, largely ignoring Hamilton's plan because it seemed so far from the general tenor of the Convention, Madison spoke at length opposing the New Jersey Plan. Immediately after his speech the Convention voted, seven states to three, with one divided, to set aside the New Jersey Plan and instead resume its consideration of the Virginia Plan.

Mr. Madison. Much stress had been laid by some gentlemen on the want of power in the Convention to propose any other than a *federal* plan. To what had been answered by others, he would only add, that neither of the characteristics attached to a *federal* plan would support this objection. One characteristic, was that in a *federal* Government, the power was exercised not on the people individually; but on the people *collectively*, on the *States*. Yet in some instances as in piracies, captures *etc.* the existing Confederacy, and in many instances, the amendments to it proposed by Mr. Paterson, must operate immediately on individuals. The other characteristic was that a *federal* Government derived its appointments not immediately from the people, but from the States which they respectively composed. Here too were facts on the other side. In two of the States, Connecticut and Rhode Island, the delegates to Congress were chosen, not by the Legislatures, but by the people at large; and the plan of Mr. Paterson intended no change in this particular.

It had been alleged [by Mr. Paterson], that the Confederation having been formed by unanimous consent, could be dissolved by unanimous Consent only. Does this doctrine result from the nature of compacts? Does it arise from any particular stipulation in the articles of Confederation? If we consider the federal union as analagous to the fundamental compact by which individuals compose one Society, and which must in its theoretic origin at least, have been the unanimous act of the component members, it can not be said that no dissolution of the compact can be effected without unanimous consent. A breach of the fundamental principles of the compact by a part of the Society would certainly absolve the other part from their obligations to it. If the breach of *any* article by *any* of the parties, does not set the others at liberty, it is because, the contrary is *implied* in the compact itself, and particularly by that law of it, which gives an indefinite authority to the majority to bind the whole in all cases. This latter circumstance shows that we are not to consider the federal Union as analagous to the social compact of individuals: for if it were so, a Majority would have a right to bind the rest, and even to form a new Constitution for the whole, which the Gentleman from New Jersey would be among the last to admit. If we consider the federal Union as analogous not to the social compacts among individual men: but to the conventions among individual States. What is the doctrine resulting from these conventions? Clearly, according to the Expositors of the law of Nations, that a breach of any one article, by any one party, leaves all the other parties at liberty, to consider the whole convention as dissolved, unless they choose rather to compel the delinquent party to repair the breach. In some treaties indeed it is expressly stipulated that a violation of particular articles shall not have this consequence, and even that particular articles shall remain in force during war, which in general is understood to dissolve all subsisting Treaties. But are there any exceptions of this sort to the Articles of confederation? So far from it that there is not even an express stipulation that force shall be used to compel an offending member of the Union to discharge its duty. He observed that the violations of the federal articles had been numerous and notorious. Among the most notorious was an act of New Jersey herself; by which she *expressly refused* to comply with a constitutional requisition of Congress and yielded no farther to the expostulations of their deputies, than barely to rescind her vote of refusal without passing any positive act of compliance. He did not wish to draw any rigid inferences from these observations. He thought it proper however that the true nature of the existing confederacy should be investigated, and he was not anxious to strengthen the foundations on which it now stands.

 Proceeding to the consideration of Mr. Paterson's plan, he stated the object of a proper plan to be twofold. 1. To preserve the Union. 2. To provide a Government that will remedy the evils felt by the States both in their united and individual capacities. Examine Mr. Paterson's plan, and say whether it promises satisfaction in these respects.

 1. Will it prevent those violations of the law of nations and of Treaties which if not prevented must involve us in the calamities of foreign wars? The tendency of the States to these violations has been manifested in sundry instances. The files of Congress contain complaints already, from almost every nation with which treaties have been formed. Hitherto indulgence has been shown to us. This can not be the permanent disposition of foreign nations. A rupture with other powers is among the greatest of national calamities. It ought therefore to be effectually provided that no part of a nation shall have it in its power to bring them on the whole. The existing Confederacy does not sufficiently provide

against this evil. The proposed amendment to it does not supply the omission. It leaves the will of the States as uncontrolled as ever.

2. Will it prevent encroachments on the federal authority? A tendency to such encroachments has been sufficiently exemplified, among ourselves, as well in every other confederated republic ancient and Modern. By the federal articles, transactions with the Indians appertain to Congress. Yet in several instances, the States have entered into treaties and wars with them. In like manner no two or more States can form among themselves any treaties *etc.* without the consent of Congress. Yet Virginia and Maryland in one instance—Pennsylvania and New Jersey in another, have entered into compacts, without previous application or subsequent apology. No State again can of right raise troops in time of peace without the like consent. Of all cases of the league, this seems to require the most scrupulous observance. Has not Massachusetts, notwithstanding, the most powerful member of the Union, already raised a body of troops? Is she not now augmenting them, without having even deigned to apprise Congress of Her intention? In fine—have we not seen the public land dealt out to Connecticut to bribe her acquiescence in the decree constitutionally awarded against her claim on the territory of Pennsylvania for no other possible motive can account for the policy of Congress in that measure?—If we recur to the examples of other confederacies, we shall find in all of them the same tendency of the parts to encroach on the authority of the whole. He then reviewed the Amphyctionic and Achæan confederacies among the ancients, and the Helvetic, Germanic and Belgic among the moderns, tracing their analogy to the United States—in the constitution and extent of their federal authorities—in the tendency of the particular members to usurp on these authorities; and to bring confusion and ruin on the whole.—He observed that the plan of Mr. Paterson besides omitting a control over the States as a general defence of the federal prerogatives was particularly defective in two of its provisions. 1. Its ratification was not to be by the people at large, but by the *legislatures.* It could not therefore render the Acts of Congress in pursuance of their powers, even legally *paramount* to the Acts of the States. 2. It gave to the federal Tribunal an appellate jurisdiction only—even in the criminal cases enumerated. The necessity of any such provision supposed a danger of undue acquittals in the State tribunals. Of what avail could an appellate tribunal be, after an acquittal? Besides in most if not all of the States, the Executives have by their respective *Constitutions* the right of pardoning. How could this be taken from them by a *legislative* ratification only?

3. Will it prevent trespasses of the States on each other? Of these enough has been already seen. He instanced Acts of Virginia and Maryland which give a preference to their own Citizens in cases where the Citizens of other States are

entitled to equality of privileges by the Articles of Confederation. He considered the emissions of paper money and other kindred measures as also aggressions. The States relatively to one another being each of them either Debtor or Creditor; the creditor States must suffer unjustly from every emission by the debtor States. We have seen retaliating acts on this subject which threatened danger not to the harmony only, but the tranquility of the Union. The plan of Mr. Paterson, not giving even a negative on the acts of the States, left them as much at liberty as ever to execute their unrighteous projects against each other.

    4. Will it secure the internal tranquility of the States themselves? The insurrections in Massachusetts admonished all the States of the danger to which they were exposed. Yet the plan of Mr. Paterson contained no provisions for supplying the defect of the Confederation on this point. According to the Republican theory indeed, Right and power being both vested in the majority, are held to be synonymous. According to fact and experience, a minority may in an appeal to force be an overmatch for the majority. 1. If the minority happen to include all such as possess the skill and habits of military life, with such as possess the great pecuniary resources, one third may conquer the remaining two thirds. 2. one third of those who participate in the choice of rulers may be rendered a majority by the accession of those whose poverty disqualifies them from a suffrage, and who for obvious reasons may be more ready to join the standard of sedition than that of the established Government. 3. where slavery exists, the Republican Theory becomes still more fallacious.

    5. Will it secure a good internal legislation and administration to the particular States? In developing the evils which vitiate the political system of the United States it is proper to take into view those which prevail within the States individually as well as those which affect them collectively: Since the former indirectly affect the whole; and there is great reason to believe that the pressure of them had a full share in the motives which produced the present Convention. Under this head he enumerated and animadverted on 1. the multiplicity of the laws passed by the several States. 2. the mutability of their laws. 3. the injustice of them. 4. the impotence of them: observing that Mr. Paterson's plan contained no remedy for this dreadful class of evils, and could not therefore be received as an adequate provision for the exigencies of the Community.

    6. Will it secure the Union against the influence of foreign powers over its members? He pretended not to say that any such influence had yet been tried: but it was naturally to be expected that occasions would produce it. As lessons which claimed particular attention, he cited the intrigues practised among the Amphyctionic Confederates first by the Kings of Persia, and afterwards fatally by Philip of Macedon: among the Achæans, first by Macedon and afterwards no

less fatally by Rome: among the Swiss by Austria, France and the lesser neighbouring powers: among the members of the Germanic Body by France, England, Spain and Russia—: and in the Belgic Republic, by all the great neighbouring powers. The plan of Mr. Paterson, not giving to the general Councils any negative on the will of the particular States, left the door open for the like pernicious machinations among ourselves.

7. He begged the smaller States which were most attached to Mr. Paterson's plan to consider the situation in which it would leave them. In the first place they would continue to bear the whole expence of maintaining their Delegates in Congress. It ought not to be said that if they were willing to bear this burden, no others had a right to complain. As far as it led the small States to forbear keeping up a representation, by which the public business was delayed, it was evidently a matter of common concern. An examination of the minutes of Congress would satisfy every one that the public business had been frequently delayed by this cause; and that the States most frequently unrepresented in Congress were not the larger States. He reminded the convention of another consequence of leaving on a small State the burden of maintaining a Representation in Congress. During a considerable period of the War, one of the Representatives of Delaware, in whom alone before the signing of the Confederation the entire vote of that State and after that event one half of its vote, frequently resided, was a Citizen and Resident of Pennsylvania and held an office in his own State incompatible with an appointment from it to Congress. During another period, the same State was represented by three delegates two of whom were citizens of Pennsylvania and the third a Citizen of New Jersey. These expedients must have been intended to avoid the burden of supporting delegates from their own State. But whatever might have been the cause, was not in effect the vote of one State doubled, and the influence of another increased by it? In the second place the coercion, on which the efficacy of the plan depends, can never be exerted but on themselves. The larger States will be impregnable, the smaller only can feel the vengeance of it. He illustrated the position by the history of the Amphyctionic Confederates: and the ban of the German Empire. It was the cobweb which could entangle the weak, but would be the sport of the strong.

8. He begged them to consider the situation in which they would remain in case their pertinacious adherence to an inadmissible plan, should prevent the adoption of any plan. The contemplation of such an event was painful; but it would be prudent to submit to the task of examining it at a distance, that the means of escaping it might be the more readily embraced. Let the Union of the States be dissolved, and one of two consequences must happen. Either the States must remain individually independent and sovereign; or two or more

Confederacies must be formed among them. In the first event would the small States be more secure against the ambition and power of their larger neighbours, than they would be under a general Government pervading with equal energy every part of the Empire, and having an equal interest in protecting every part against every other part? In the second, can the smaller expect that their larger neighbours would confederate with them on the principle of the present confederacy, which gives to each member, an equal suffrage; or that they would exact less severe concessions from the smaller States, than are proposed in the scheme of Mr. Randolph?

The great difficulty lies in the affair of Representation; and if this could be adjusted, all others would be surmountable. It was admitted by both the gentlemen from New Jersey [Mr. Brearly and Mr. Paterson], that it would not be *just to allow Virginia* which was 16 times as large as Delaware an equal vote only. Their language was that it would not be *safe for Delaware* to allow Virginia 16 times as many votes. The expedient proposed by them was that all the States should be thrown into one mass and a new partition be made into 13 equal parts. Would such a scheme be practicable? The dissimilarities existing in the rules of property, as well as in the manners, habits and prejudices of the different States, amounted to a prohibition of the attempt. It had been found impossible for the power of one of the most absolute princes in Europe [King of France] directed by the wisdom of one of the most enlightened and patriotic Ministers [Mr. Neckar] that any age has produced to equalize in some points only the different usages and regulations of the different provinces. But admitting a general amalgamation and repartition of the States to be practicable, and the danger apprehended by the smaller States from a proportional representation to be real; would not a particular and voluntary coalition of these with their neighbours, be less inconvenient to the whole community, and equally effectual for their own safety. If New Jersey or Delaware conceived that an advantage would accrue to them from an equalization of the States, in which case they would necessarily form a junction with their neighbours, why might not this end be attained by leaving them at liberty by the Constitution to form such a junction whenever they pleased? And why should they wish to obtrude a like arrangement on all the States, when it was, to say the least, extremely difficult, would be obnoxious to many of the States, and when neither the inconveniency, nor the benefit of the expedient to themselves, would be lessened, by confining it to themselves.—The prospect of many new States to the Westward was another consideration of importance. If they should come into the Union at all, they would come when they contained but few inhabitants. If they should be entitled to vote according to their proportions of inhabitants, all would be right and safe. Let them have an equal vote, and a more objectionable minority than ever might give law to the whole.

Debate on Federalism (June 21)

As the Convention in plenary session considered one by one the resolves based on the Virginia Plan, most of the debate was on technical and practical matters rather than on points of principle, but occasionally more basic arguments surfaced. William Johnson of Connecticut, Wilson, and Madison exchanged views on the tendencies of the state and national governments to encroach on each other.

DR. JOHNSON. On a comparison of the two plans which had been proposed from Virginia and New Jersey, it appeared that the peculiarity which characterized the latter was its being calculated to preserve the individuality of the States. The plan from Virginia did not profess to destroy this individuality altogether, but was charged with such a tendency. One Gentleman alone (Colonel Hamilton) in his animadversions on the plan of New Jersey, boldly and decisively contended for an abolition of the State Governments. Mr. Wilson and the gentlemen from Virginia who also were adversaries of the plan of New Jersey held a different language. They wished to leave the States in possession of a considerable, though a subordinate jurisdiction. They had not yet however shown how this could consist with, or be secured against the general sovereignty and jurisdiction, which they proposed to give to the national Government. If this could be shown in such a manner as to satisfy the patrons of the New Jersey propositions, that the individuality of the States would not be endangered, many of their objections would no doubt be removed. If this could not be shown their objections would have their full force. He wished it therefore to be well considered whether in case the States, as was proposed, should retain some portion of sovereignty at least, this portion could be preserved, without allowing them to participate effectually in the General Government, without giving them each a distinct and equal vote for the purpose of defending themselves in the general Councils.

MR. WILSON'S respect for Dr. Johnson, added to the importance of the subject led him to attempt, unprepared as he was, to solve the difficulty which had been started. It was asked how the General Government and individuality of the particular States could be reconciled to each other; and how the latter could be secured against the former? Might it not, on the other side be asked how the former was to be secured against the latter? It was generally admitted that a jealousy and [rivalry] would be felt between the General and particular Governments. As the plan now stood, though indeed contrary to his opinion, one branch of the General Government (the Senate or second branch) was to be appointed by the State Legislatures. The State Legislatures, therefore, by this participation in the General Government would have an opportunity of defending their rights. Ought not a reciprocal opportunity to be given to the General Government of defending itself by having an appointment of some one constituent branch of the State Government. If a security be necessary on one side, it would seem reasonable to demand it on the other. But taking the matter in a more general view, he saw no danger to the States from the General Government. In case a combination should be made by the large ones it would produce a general alarm among the rest; and the project would be frustrated. But there was no temptation to such a project. The States having in general a similar interest, in case of any proposition in the National Legislature to encroach on the State Legislatures, he conceived a general alarm would take place in the National Legislature itself, that it would communicate itself to the State Legislatures, and would finally spread among the people at large. The General Government will be as ready to preserve the rights of the States as the latter are to preserve the rights of individuals; all the members of the former, having a common interest, as representatives of all the people of the latter, to leave the State Governments in possession of what the people wish them to retain. He could not discover, therefore any danger whatever on the side from which it had been apprehended. On the contrary, he conceived that in spite of every precaution the general Government would be in perpetual danger of encroachments from the State Governments.

 Mr. Madison was of opinion that there was 1. less danger of encroachment from the General Government than from the State Government. 2. That the mischief from encroachments would be less fatal if made by the former, than if made by the latter. 1. All the examples of other confederacies prove the greater tendency in such systems to anarchy than to tyranny; to a disobedience of the members than to usurpations of the federal head. Our own experience had fully illustrated this tendency.—But it will be said that the proposed change in the principles and form of the Union will vary the tendency; that the General Governments will have real and greater powers, and will be derived in one branch at least from the people, not from the Government of the States. To give full force to this objection, let it be supposed for a moment that indefinite power should be given to the General Legislature, and the States reduced to corporations dependent on the General Legislature; why should it follow that the General Government would take from the States any branch of their power as far as its operation was beneficial, and its continuance desirable to the people? In some of the States, particularly in Connecticut, all the Townships are incorporated, and have a certain limited jurisdiction. Have the Representatives of the people of the Townships in the Legislature of the State ever endeavored to despoil the Townships of any part of their local authority? As far as this local authority is convenient to the people they are attached to it; and their representatives chosen by and amenable to them naturally respect their attachment to this, as much as their attachment to any other right or interest. The relation of a General Government to State Governments is parallel. 2. Guards were more necessary against encroachments of the State Governments on the General Government than of the latter on the former. The great objection made against an abolition of the State Government was that the General Government could not extend its care to all the minute objects which fall under the cognizance of the local jurisdictions. The objection as stated lay not against the probable abuse of the general power, but against the imperfect use that could be made of it throughout so great an extent of country, and over so great a variety of objects. As far as its operation would be practicable it could not in this view be improper; as far as it would be impracticable, the conveniency of the General Government itself would concur with that of the people in the maintenance of subordinate Governments. Were it practicable for the General Government to extend its care to every requisite object without the cooperation of the State Governments the people would not be less free as members of one great Republic than as members of thirteen small ones. A Citizen of Delaware was not more free than a Citizen of Virginia: nor would either be more free than a Citizen of America. Supposing therefore a tendency in the General Government to absorb the State Governments no fatal consequence could result. Taking the reverse of the supposition, that a tendency should be left in the State Governments towards an independence on the General Government and the gloomy consequences need not be pointed out. The imagination of them, must have suggested to the States the experiment we are now making to prevent the calamity, and must have formed the chief motive with those present to undertake the arduous task.

Length of Term in Office for Senators (June 26)

After three days discussing details, the Convention debated the length of term for Senators. The issue provoked Madison, Roger Sherman, and Hamilton to open a basic question: were long or short terms more likely to result in wise decisions that would protect the interests of the people?

MR. MADISON. In order to judge of the form to be given to this institution, it will be proper to take a view of the ends to be served by it. These were first to protect the people against their rulers: secondly to protect the people against the transient impressions into which they themselves might be led. A people deliberating in a temperate moment, and with the experience of other nations before them, on the plan of Government most likely to secure their happiness, would first be aware, that those charged with the public happiness, might betray their trust. An obvious precaution against this danger would be to divide the trust between different bodies of men, who might watch and check each other. In this they would be governed by the same prudence which has prevailed in organizing the subordinate departments of Government, where all business liable to abuses is made to pass through separate hands, the one being a check on the other. It would next occur to such a people, that they themselves were liable to temporary errors, through want of information as to their true interest, and that men chosen for a short term, and employed but a small portion of that in public affairs, might err from the same cause. This reflection would naturally suggest that the Government be so constituted, as that one of its branches might have an opportunity of acquiring a competent knowledge of the public interests. Another reflection equally becoming a people on such an occasion, would be that they themselves, as well as a numerous body of Representatives, were liable to err also, from fickleness and passion. A necessary fence against this danger would be to select a portion of enlightened citizens, whose limited number, and firmness might seasonably interpose against impetuous councils. It ought finally to occur to a people deliberating on a Government for themselves, that as different interests necessarily result from the liberty meant to be secured, the major interest might under sudden impulses be tempted to commit injustice on the minority. In all civilized Countries the people fall into different classes having a real or supposed difference of interests. There will be creditors and debtors, farmers, merchants and manufacturers. There will be particularly the distinction of rich and poor. It was true as had been observed [by Mr. Pinckney] we had not among us those hereditary distinctions, of rank which were a great source of the contests in the ancient Governments as well as the modern States of Europe, nor those extremes of wealth or poverty which characterize the latter. We cannot however be regarded even at this time, as one homogeneous mass, in which every thing that affects a part will affect in the same manner the whole. In framing a system which we wish to last for ages, we should not lose sight of the changes which ages will produce. An increase of population will of necessity increase the proportion of those who will labour under all the hardships of life, and secretly sigh for a more equal distribution of its blessings. These may in time outnumber those who are placed above the feelings of indigence. According to the equal laws of suffrage, the power will slide into the hands of the former. No agrarian attempts have yet been made in this Country, but symptoms, of a leveling spirit, as we have understood, have sufficiently appeared in a certain quarters to give notice of the future danger. How is this danger to be guarded against on republican principles? How is the danger in all cases of interested coalitions to oppress the minority to be guarded against? Among other means by the establishment of a body in the Government sufficiently respectable for its wisdom and virtue, to aid on such emergences, the preponderance of justice by throwing its weight into that scale. Such being the objects of the second branch in the proposed Government he thought a considerable duration ought to be given to it. He did not conceive that the term of nine years could threaten any real danger; but in pursuing his particular ideas on the subject, he should require that the long term allowed to the second branch should not commence till such a period of life, as would render a perpetual disqualification to be re-elected little inconvenient either in a public or private view. He observed that as it was more than probable we were now digesting a plan which in its operation would decide for ever the fate of Republican Government we ought not only to provide every guard to liberty that its preservation could require, but be equally careful to supply the defects which our own experience had particularly pointed out.

    MR. SHERMAN. Government is instituted for those who live under it. It ought therefore to be so constituted as not to be dangerous to their liberties. The more permanency it has the worse if it be a bad Government. Frequent elections are necessary to preserve the good behavior of rulers. They also tend to give permanency to the Government, by preserving that good behavior, because it ensures their re-election. In Connecticut elections have been very frequent, yet great stability and uniformity both as to persons and measures have been experienced from its original establishment to the present time; a period of more than 130 years. He wished to have provision made for steadiness and wisdom in the system to be adopted; but he thought six or four years would be sufficient. He should be content with either.

MR. READ wished it to be considered by the small States that it was their interest that we should become one people as much as possible; that State attachments should be extinguished as much as possible; that the Senate should be so constituted as to have the feelings of Citizens of the whole.

MR. HAMILTON. He did not mean to enter particularly into the subject. He concurred with Mr. Madison in thinking we were now to decide for ever the fate of Republican Government; and that if we did not give to that form due stability and wisdom, it would be disgraced and lost among ourselves, disgraced and lost to mankind for ever. He acknowledged himself not to think favorably of Republican Government; but addressed his remarks to those who did think favorably of it, in order to prevail on them to tone their Government as high as possible. He professed himself to be as zealous an advocate for liberty as any man whatever, and trusted he should be as willing a martyr to it though he differed as to the form in which it was most eligible.—He concurred also in the general observations of [Mr. Madison] on the subject, which might be supported by others if it were necessary. It was certainly true: that nothing like an equality of property existed: that an inequality would exist as long as liberty existed, and that it would unavoidably result from that very liberty itself. This inequality of property constituted the great and fundamental distinction in Society. When the Tribunitial power had levelled the boundary between the *patricians and plebeians*, what followed? The distinction between rich and poor was substituted. He meant not however to enlarge on the subject. He rose principally to remark that [Mr. Sherman] seemed not to recollect that one branch of the proposed government was so formed, as to render it particularly the guardians of the poorer orders of Citizens; nor to have adverted to the true causes of the stability which had been exemplified in Connecticut. Under the British system as well as the federal, many of the great powers appertaining to Government particularly all those relating to foreign Nations were not in the hands of the Government there. Their internal affairs also were extremely simple, owing to sundry causes many of which were peculiar to that Country. Of late the Government had entirely given way to the people, and had in fact suspended many of its ordinary functions in order to prevent those turbulent scenes which had appeared elsewhere. He asks Mr. S. whether the State at this time, dare impose and collect a tax on the people? To these causes and not to the frequency of elections, the effect, as far as it existed ought to be chiefly ascribed.

Debate on State Equality in the Senate (June 28-July 2)

Debate, though, resumed on the most divisive issue before the Convention: should the states have an equal vote in the upper house of the legislature (the Senate)? Madison, Wilson, and other delegates (mostly from large states) opposed state equality because the states themselves were so unequal in size. Equality in the Senate would thus violate the fundamental republican principle of government according to the equal voices of the people consenting to be governed. A series of increasingly vehement speeches over a five-day period (June 28-July 2) revealed bitter rivalry. Madison, Wilson, Rufus King of Massachusetts, and Gouverneur Morris of Pennsylvania argued against state equality in the Senate, while William Samuel Johnson and Oliver Ellsworth of Connecticut and Gunning Bedford of Delaware advocated such equality. Bedford's speech is from the notes of Robert Yates, and is reprinted from C. C. Tansill, ed., Documents, *pp. 834-836.*

...MR. MADISON. Why are counties of the same states represented in proportion to their numbers? Is it because the representatives are chosen by the people themselves? So will be the representatives in the National Legislature. Is it because the larger have more at stake than the smaller? The case will be the same with the larger and smaller States. Is it because the laws are to operate immediately on their persons and properties? The same is the case in some degree as the articles of confederation stand; the same will be the case in a far greater degree under the plan proposed to be substituted. In the cases of captures, of piracies, and of offences in a federal army; the property and persons of individuals depend on the laws of Congress. By the plan proposed a compleat power of taxation, the highest prerogative of supremacy is proposed to be vested in the National Government. Many other powers are added which assimilate it to the Government of individual States. The negative proposed on the State laws, will make it an essential branch of the State Legislatures and of course will require that it should be exercised by a body established on like principles with the other branches of those Legislatures.—That it is not necessary to secure the small States against the large ones he conceived to be equally obvious: Was a combination of the large ones dreaded? This must arise either from some interest common to Virginia, Massachusetts and Pennsylvania and distinguishing them from the other States or from the mere circumstance of similarity of size. Did any such common interest exist? In point of situation they could not have been more effectually separated from each other by the most jealous citizen of the most jealous State. In point of manners, Religion, and the other circumstances which sometimes beget affection between different communities, they were not more assimilated than the other States.—In point of the staple productions they were as dissimilar as any three other States in the Union. The Staple of Massachusetts was *fish*, of Pennsylvania *flour*, of Virginia *Tobacco*. Was a combination to be apprehended from the mere circumstance of equality of size? Experience suggested no such danger. The journals of Congress did not present any peculiar association of these States in the votes recorded. It had never been seen that different Counties in the same State, conformable in extent, but disagreeing in other circumstances, betrayed a propensity to such combinations. Experience rather taught a contrary lesson. Among individuals of superior eminence and weight in Society, rivalships were much more frequent than coalitions. Among independent nations, pre-eminent over their neighbours, the same remark was verified. Carthage and Rome tore one another to pieces instead of uniting their forces to devour the weaker nations of the Earth. The Houses of Austria and France were hostile as long as they remained the greatest powers of Europe. England and France have succeeded to the pre-eminence and to the enmity. To this principle we owe perhaps our liberty. A coalition between those powers would have been fatal to us. Among the principal members of ancient and Modern confederacies, we find the same effect from the same cause. The contentions, not the Coalitions of Sparta, Athens and Thebes, proved fatal to the smaller members of the Amphyctionic Confederacy. The contentions, not the combinations of Prussia and Austria, have distracted and oppressed the Germanic empire. Were the large States formidable *singly* to their smaller neighbours? On this supposition the latter ought to wish for such a general Government as will operate with equal energy on the former as on themselves. The more lax the band, the more liberty the larger will have to avail themselves of their superior force. Here again Experience was an instructive monitor. What is the situation of the weak compared with the strong in those stages of civilization in which the violence of individuals is least controled by an efficient Government? The Heroic period of Ancient Greece, the feudal licentiousness of the middle ages of Europe, the existing condition of the American Savages, answer this question. What is the situation of the minor sovereigns in the great society of independent nations, in which the more powerful are under no control but the nominal authority of the law of Nations? Is not the danger to the former exactly in proportion to their weakness? But there are cases still more in point. What was the condition of the weaker members of the Amphyctionic Confederacy. Plutarch [life of Themistocles] will inform us that it happened but too often that the strongest cities corrupted and awed the weaker, and that Judgment went in favor of the more powerful party. What is the condition of the lesser states in the German Confederacy? We all know that they are exceedingly trampled upon; and that they owe their safety as far as they enjoy it, partly to their enlisting themselves, under the rival banners of the pre-eminent members, partly to alliances with neighbouring Princes which the Consitution of the Empire does not prohibit. What is the state of things in the lax system of the Dutch Confederacy? Holland contains about one half the people, supplies about one half of the money, and by her influence, silently and indirectly governs the whole republic. In a word, the two extremes before us are a perfect separation and a perfect incorporation, of the 13 States. In the first case they would be independent nations subject to no law, but the law of nations. In the last, they would be mere counties of one entire republic, subject to one common law. In the first case the smaller States would have every thing to fear from the larger. In the last they would have nothing to fear. The true policy of the small States therefore lies in promoting those principles and that form of Government which will most approximate the States to the condition of counties. Another consideration may be added. If the General Government be feeble, the large States distrusting its continuance, and foreseeing that their importance and security may depend on their own size and strength, will never submit to a partition. Give to the General Government sufficient energy and permanency, and you remove the objection. Gradual partitions of the large, and junctions of the small States will be facilitated, and time may effect that equalization, which is wished for by the small States now, but can never be accomplished at once....

    DR. JOHNSON. The controversy must be endless whilst Gentlemen differ in the grounds of their arguments: Those on one side considering the States as districts of people composing one political Society; those on the other considering them as so many political societies. The fact is that the States do exist as political Societies, and a Government is to be formed for them in their political capacity, as well as for the individuals composing them. Does it not seem to follow, that if the States as such are to exist they must be armed with some power of self-defence. This is the idea of [Colonel Mason] who appears to have looked to the bottom of this matter. Besides the Aristocratic and other interests, which ought to have the means of defending themselves, the States have their interests as such, and are equally entitled to like means. On the whole he thought that as in some respects the States are to be considered in their political capacity, and in others as districts of individual citizens, the two ideas embraced on different sides, instead of being opposed to each other, ought to be combined; that in *one* branch the *people,* ought to be represented; in the *other* the *States*....

Mr. MADISON agreed with Dr. Johnson, that the mixed nature of the Government ought to be kept in view; but thought too much stress was laid on the rank of the States as political societies. There was a gradation, he observed, from the smallest corporation, with the most limited powers, to the largest empire with the most perfect sovereignty. He pointed out the limitations on the sovereignty of the States, as now confederated their laws in relation to the paramount law of the Confederacy were analogous to that of bye laws to the supreme law within a State. Under the proposed Government the powers of the States will be much farther reduced. According to the views of every member, the General Government will have powers far beyond those exercised by the British Parliament, when the States were part of the British Empire. It will in particular have the power, without the consent of the State Legislatures, to levy money directly on the people themselves; and therefore not to divest such *unequal* portions of the people as composed the several States, of an *equal* voice, would subject the system to the reproaches and evils which have resulted from the vicious representation in Great Britain.

He entreated the gentlemen representing the small States to renounce a principle which was confessedly unjust, which could never be admitted, and if admitted must infuse mortality into a Constitution which we wished to last forever. He prayed them to ponder well the consequences of suffering the Confederacy to go to pieces. It had been said that the want of energy in the large states would be a security to the small. It was forgotten that this want of energy proceeded from the supposed security of the States against all external danger. Let each state depend on itself for its security, and let apprehensions arise of danger, from distant powers or from neighbouring States, and the languishing condition of all the States, large as well as small, would soon be transformed into vigorous and high toned Government. His great fear was that their Governments would then have too much energy, that these might not only be formidable in the large to the small States, but fatal to the internal liberty of all. The same causes which have rendered the old world the Theatre of incessant wars, and have banished liberty from the face of it, would soon produce the same effects here. The weakness and jealousy of the small States would quickly introduce some regular military force against sudden danger from their powerful neighbours. The example would be followed by others, and would soon become universal. In time of actual war, great discretionary powers are constantly given to the

Executive Magistrate. Constant apprehension of war, has the same tendency to render the head too large for the body. A standing military force, with an overgrown Executive will not long be safe companions to liberty. The means of defence against foreign danger, have been always the instruments of tyranny at home. Among the Romans it was a standing maxim to excite a war, whenever a revolt was apprehended. Throughout all Europe, the armies kept up under the pretext of defending, have enslaved the people. It is perhaps questionable, whether the best concerted system of absolute power in Europe could maintain itself, in a situation, where no alarms of external danger could tame the people to the domestic yoke. The insular situation of Great Britain was the principal cause of her being an exception to the general fate of Europe. It has rendered less defence necessary, and admitted a kind of defence which could not be used for the purpose of oppression.—These consequences he conceived ought to be apprehended whether the States should run into a total separation from each other, or should enter into partial confederacies. Either event would be truly deplorable; and those who might be accessary to either, could never be forgiven by their Country, nor by themselves.

MR. HAMILTON observed that individuals forming political Societies modify their rights differently, with regard to suffrage. Examples of it are found in all the States. In all of them some individuals are deprived of the right altogether, not having the requisite qualification of property. In some of the States the right of suffrage is allowed in some cases and refused in others. To vote for a member in one branch, a certain quantum of property, to vote for a member in another branch of the Legislature, a higher quantum of property is required. In like manner States may modify their right of suffrage differently, the larger exercising a larger, the smaller a smaller share of it. But as States are a collection of individual men which ought we to respect most, the rights of the people composing them, or of the artificial beings resulting from the composition. Nothing could be more preposterous or absurd than to sacrifice the former to the latter. It has been said that if the smaller States renounce their *equality*, they renounce at the same time their *liberty*. The truth is it is a contest for power, not for liberty. Will the men composing the small States be less free than those composing the larger. The State of Delaware having 40,000 souls will *lose power*, if she has one tenth only of the votes allowed to Pennsylvania having 400,000: but will the people of Delaware *be less free*, if each citizen has an equal vote with each citizen of Pennsylvania. He admitted that common residence within the same State would produce a certain degree of attachment; and that this principle might have a certain influence in public affairs. He thought however that this might by some precautions be in a great measure excluded:

and that no material inconvenience could result from it, as there could not be any ground for combination among the States whose influence was most dreaded. The only considerable distinction of interests, lay between the carrying and noncarrying States, which divide instead of uniting the largest States. No considerable inconvenience had been found from the division of the State of New York into different districts of different sizes.

Some of the consequences of a dissolution of the Union, and the establishment of partial confederacies, had been pointed out. He would add another of a most serious nature. Alliances will immediately be formed with different rival and hostile nations of Europe, who will foment disturbances among ourselves, and make us parties to all their own quarrels. Foreign Nations having American dominions are and must be jealous of us. Their representatives betray the utmost anxiety for our fate, and for the result of this meeting, which must have an essential influence on it.—It had been said that respectability in the eyes of foreign Nations was not the object at which we aimed; that the proper object of republican Government was domestic tranquility and happiness. This was an ideal distinction. No Government could give us tranquility and happiness at home, which did not possess sufficient stability and strength to make us respectable abroad. This was the critical moment for forming such a Government. We should run every risk in trusting to future amendments. As yet we retain the habits of union. We are weak and sensible of our weakness. Henceforward the motives will become feebler, and the difficulties greater. It is a miracle that we were now here exercising our tranquil and free deliberations on the subject. It would be madness to trust to future miracles. A thousand causes must obstruct a reproduction of them....

MR. ELLSWORTH moved that the rule of suffrage in the second branch be the same with that established by the articles of confederation. He was not sorry on the whole he said that the vote just passed, had determined against this rule in the first branch. He hoped it would become a ground of compromise with regard to the second branch. We were partly national; partly federal. The proportional representation in the first branch was conformable to the national principle and would secure the large States against the small. An equality of voices was conformable to the federal principle and was necessary to secure the Small States against the large. He trusted that on this middle ground a compromise would take place. He did not see that it could on any other. And if no compromise should take place, our meeting would not only be in vain but worse than in vain. To the Eastward he was sure Massachusetts was the only State that would listen to a proposition for excluding the States as equal political Societies, from an equal voice in both branches. The others would risk every consequence rather than part with so dear a right. An attempt to deprive them of it, was at once cutting the body of America in two, and as he supposed would be the case, somewhere about this part of it. The large States he conceived would notwithstanding the equality of votes, have an influence that would maintain their superiority. Holland, as had been admitted [by Mr. Madison] had, notwithstanding a like equality in the Dutch Confederacy, a prevailing influence in the public measures. The power of self-defence was essential to the small States. Nature had given it to the smallest insect of the creation. He could never admit that there was no danger of combinations among the large States. They will like individuals find out and avail themselves of the advantage to be gained by it. It was true the danger would be greater, if they were contiguous and had a more immediate common interest. A defensive combination of the small States was rendered more difficult by their greater number. He would mention another consideration of great weight. The existing confederation was founded on the equality of the States in the article of suffrage: was it meant to pay no regard to this antecedent plighted faith. Let a strong Executive, a Judiciary and Legislative power be created; but let not too much be attempted; by which all may be lost. He was not in general a half-way man, yet he preferred doing half the good we could, rather than do nothing at all. The other half may be added, when the necessity shall be more fully experienced....

MR. WILSON did not expect such a motion after the establishment of the contrary principle in the first branch; and considering the reasons which would oppose it, even if an equal vote had been allowed in the first branch. The Gentleman from Connecticut [Mr. Ellsworth] had pronounced that if the motion should not be acceded to, of all the States North of Pennsylvania one only would agree to any General Government. He entertained more favorable hopes of Connecticut and of the other Northern States. He hoped the alarms exceeded their cause, and that they would not abandon a Country to which they were bound by so many strong and endearing ties. But should the deplored event happen, it would neither stagger his sentiments nor his duty. If the minority of the people of America refuse to coalesce with the majority on just the proper principles, if a separation must take place, it could never happen on better grounds. The votes of yesterday against the just principle of representation, were as 22 to 90 of the people of America. Taking the opinions to be the same on this point, and he was sure if there was any room for change, it could not be on the side of the majority, the question will be shall less than one quarter of the United States withdraw themselves from the Union; or shall more than three quarters renounce the inherent, indisputable, and unalienable rights of men, in favor of the artificial systems of States. If issue must be joined, it was on this point he would choose to join it. The gentleman from Connecticut in supposing that the preponderancy secured to the majority in the first branch had removed the objections to an equality of votes in the second branch for the security of the minority, narrowed the case extremely. Such an equality will enable the minority to control in all cases whatsoever, the sentiments and interests of the majority. Seven States will control six: Seven States, according to the estimates that had been used, composed twenty-four ninetieths of the whole people. It would be in the power then of less than one third to overrule two thirds whenever a question should happen to divide the States in that manner. Can we forget for whom we are forming a Government? Is it for *men*, or for the imaginary beings called *States?* Will our honest Constituents be satisfied with metaphysical distinctions? Will they, ought they to be satisfied with being told that the one third compose the greater number of States? The rule of suffrage ought on every principle to be the same in the second as in the first branch. If the Government be not laid on this foundation, it can be neither solid nor lasting. Any other principle will be local, confined and temporary. This will expand with the expansion, and grow with the growth of the United States.—Much has been said of an imaginary combination of three States. Sometimes a danger of monarchy, sometimes of aristocracy, has been charged on it. No explanation however of the danger has been vouchsafed. It would be easy to prove both from reason and history that rivalships would be more probable than coalitions; and that there are no coinciding interests that could produce the latter. No answer has yet been given to the observations of [Mr. Madison] on this subject. Should the Executive Magistrate be taken from one of the large States would not the other two be thereby thrown into the scale with the other States? Whence then the danger of monarchy? Are the people of the three large States more aristocratic than those of the small ones? Whence then the danger of aristocracy from their influence? It is all a mere illusion of names. We talk of States, till we forget what they are composed of. Is a real and fair majority, the natural hot-bed of aristocracy? It is a part of the definition of this species of Government or rather of tyranny, that the smaller number governs the greater. It is true that a majority of States in the second branch can not carry a law against a majority of the people in the first. But this removes half only of the objection. Bad Governments are of two sorts. 1. that which does too little. 2. that which does too much: that which fails through weakness; and that which destroys through oppression. Under which of these evils do the United States at present groan? under the weakness and inefficiency of its Government. To remedy this weakness we have been sent to this Convention. If the motion should be agreed to, we shall leave the United States fettered precisely as heretofore; with the additional mortification of seeing the good purposes of the fair representation of the people in the first branch, defeated in second. Twenty four will still control sixty six. He lamented that such a disagreement should prevail on the point of representation, as he did not foresee that it would happen on the other point most contested, the boundary between the General and the local authorities. He thought the States necessary and valuable parts of a good system.

Mr. Ellsworth. The capital objection of Mr. Wilson "that the minority will rule the majority" is not true. The power is given to the few to save them from being destroyed by the many. If an equality of votes had been given to them in both branches, the objection might have had weight. Is it a novel thing that the few should have a check on the many? Is it not the case in the British Constitution the wisdom of which so many gentlemen have united in applauding? Have not the House of Lords, who form so small a proportion of the nation a negative on the laws, as a necessary defence of their peculiar rights against the encroachment of the Commons. No instance of a Confederacy has existed in which an equality of voices has not been exercised by the members of it. We are running from one extreme to another. We are razing the foundations of the building, when we need only repair the roof. No salutary measure has been lost for want of *a majority of the States*, to favor it. If security be all that the great States wish for the first branch secures them. The danger of combinations among them is not imaginary. Although no particular abuses could be foreseen by him, the possibility of them would be sufficient to alarm him. But he could easily conceive cases in which they might result from such combinations. Suppose that in pursuance of some commercial treaty or arrangement, three or four free ports and no more were to be established would not combinations be formed in favor of Boston, Philadelphia, and some port in Chesapeak? A like concert might be formed in the appointment of the great officers. He appealed again to the obligations of the federal pact which was still in force, and which had been entered into with so much solemnity; persuading himself that some regard would still be paid to the plighted faith under which each State small as well as great, held an equal right of suffrage in the general Councils. His remarks were not the result of partial or local views. The State he represented [Connecticut] held a middle rank.

Mr. Madison did justice to the able and close reasoning of Mr. Ellsworth but must observe that it did not always accord with itself. On another occasion, the large States were described by him as the Aristocratic States, ready to oppress the small. Now the small are the House of Lords requiring a negative to defend them against the more numerous commons. Mr. Ellsworth had also erred in saying that no instance had existed in which confederated States had not retained to themselves a perfect equality of suffrage. Passing over the German system in which the King of Prussia has nine voices, he reminded Mr. Ellsworth of the Lycian confederacy, in which the component members had votes proportioned to their importance, and which Montesquieu recommends as the fittest model for that form of Government. Had the fact been as stated by Mr. Ellsworth it would have been of little avail to him, or rather would have strengthened the arguments against him; the History and fate of the several confederacies modern as well as Ancient, demonstrating some radical vice in their structure. In reply to the appeal of Mr. Ellsworth to the faith plighted in the existing federal compact, he remarked that the party claiming from others an adherence to a common engagement ought at least to be guiltless itself of a violation. Of all the States however Connecticut was perhaps least able to urge this plea. Besides the various omissions to perform the stipulated acts from which no State was free, the Legislature of that State had by a pretty recent vote, *positively, refused* to pass a law for complying with the Requisitions of Congress and had transmitted a copy of the vote to Congress. It was urged, he said, continually that an equality of votes in the second branch was not only necessary to secure the small, but would be perfectly safe to the large ones whose majority in the first branch was an effectual bulwark. But notwithstanding this apparent defence, the majority of States might still injure the majority of people. 1. They could *obstruct* the wishes and interests of the majority. 2. They could *extort* measures repugnant to the wishes and interest of the majority. 3. They could *impose* measures adverse thereto; as the second branch will probly exercise some great powers, in which the first will not participate. He admitted that every peculiar interest whether in any class of citizens, or any description of States, ought to be secured as far as possible. Wherever there is danger of attack there ought to be given a constitutional power of defence. But he contended that the States were divided into different interests not by their difference of size, but by other circumstances; the most material of which resulted partly from climate, but principally from the effects of their having or not having slaves. These two causes concurred in forming the great division of interests in the United States. It did not lie between the large and small States: It lay between the Northern and Southern, and if any defensive power were necessary, it ought to be mutually given to these two interests. He was so strongly impressed with this important truth that he had been casting about in his mind for some expedient that would answer the purpose. The one which had occurred was that instead of proportioning the votes of the States in both branches, to their respective numbers of inhabitants computing the slaves in the ratio of 5 to 3, they should be represented in one branch according to the number of free inhabitants only; and in the other according to the whole number counting the slaves as if free. By this arrangement the Southern Scale would have the advantage in one House, and the Northern in the other. He had been restrained from proposing this expedient by two considerations: one was his unwillingness to urge any diversity of interests on an occasion where it is but too apt to arise of itself—the other was, the inequality of powers that must be vested in the two branches, and which would destroy the equilibrium of interests....

MR. KING observed that the simple question was whether each State should have an equal vote in the second branch; that it must be apparent to those gentlemen who liked neither the motion for this equality, nor the report as it stood, that the report was as susceptible of melioration as the motion; that a reform would be nugatory and nominal only if we should make another Congress of the proposed Senate: that if the adherence to an equality of votes was fixed and unalterable, there could not be less obstinacy on the other side, and that we were in fact cut asunder already, and it was in vain to shut our eyes against it: that he was however filled with astonishment that if we were convinced that every *man* in America was secured in all his rights, we should be ready to sacrifice this substantial good to the phantom of *State* sovereignty: that his feelings were more harrowed and his fears more agitated for his Country than he could express, that he conceived this to be the last opportunity of providing for its liberty and happiness: that he could not therefore but repeat his amazement that when a just Government founded on a fair representation of the *people* of America was within our reach, we should renounce the blessing, from an attachment to the ideal freedom and importance of *States:* that should this wonderful illusion continue to prevail, his mind was prepared for every event, rather than to sit down under a Government founded in a vicious principle of representation, and which must be as short lived as it would be unjust.

MR. BEDFORD. That all the states at present are equally sovereign and independent, has been asserted from every quarter of this house. Our deliberations here are a confirmation of the position; and I may add to it, that each of them act from interested, and many from ambitious motives. Look at the votes which have been given on the floor of this house, and it will be found that their numbers, wealth and local views, have actuated their determinations; and that the larger states proceed as if our eyes were already perfectly blinded. Impartiality, with them, is already out of the question—the reported plan is their political creed, and they support it, right or wrong. Even the diminutive state of Georgia has an eye to her future wealth and greatness—South Carolina, puffed up with the possession of her wealth and negroes, and North Carolina, are all, from different views, united with the great states. And these latter, although it is said they can never, from interested views, form a coalition, we find closely united in one scheme of interest and ambition, notwithstanding they endeavor to amuse us with the purity of their principles and the rectitude of their intentions, in asserting that the general government must be drawn from an equal representation of the people. Pretences to support ambition are never wanting. Their cry is, where is the danger? and they insist that altho' the powers of the general government will be increased, yet it will be for the good of the whole; and although the three great states form nearly a majority of the people of America, they never will hurt or injure the lesser states. *I do not, gentlemen, trust you.* If you possess the power, the abuse of it could not be checked; and what then would prevent you from exercising it to our destruction? You gravely alledge that there is no danger of combination, and triumphantly ask, how could combinations be affected? "The larger states," you say, "all differ in productions and commerce; and experience shows that instead of combinations, they would be rivals, and counteract the views of one another." This, I repeat, is language calculated only to amuse us. Yes, sir, the larger states will be rivals, but not against each other—they will be rivals against the *rest of the states.* But it is urged that such a government would suit the people, and that its principles are equitable and just. How often has this argument been refuted, when applied to a *federal* government. The small states never can agree to the Virginia plan; and why then is it still urged? But it is said that it is not expected that the state governments will approve the proposed system, and that this house must directly carry it to THE PEOPLE for their approbation! Is it come to this, then, that *the sword* must decide this controversy, and that the horrors of war must be added to the rest of our misfortunes? But what have the people already said? "We find the confederation defective—go, and give additional powers to the confederation—give to it the imposts, regulation of trade, power to collect the taxes, and the means to discharge our foreign and domestic debts." Can we not then, as their delegates, agree upon these points? As their ambassadors, can we not clearly grant those powers? Why then, when we are met, must entire, distinct, and new grounds be taken, and a government, of which the people had no idea, be instituted? And are we to be told, if we won't agree to it, it is the last moment of our deliberations? I say, it is indeed the last moment, if we do agree to this assumption of power. The states will never again be entrapped into a measure like this. The people will say the *small* states would confederate, and grant further powers to Congress; but you, the *large* states, would not. Then the fault will be yours, and all the nations of the earth will justify us. But what is to become of our public debts if we dissolve the union? Where is your plighted faith? Will you crush the smaller states, or must they be left unmolested? Sooner than be ruined, there are *foreign powers who will take us by the hand.* I say not this to threaten or intimidate, but that we should reflect seriously before we act. If we once leave this floor, and solemnly renounce your new project, what will be the consequence? You will annihilate your federal government, and ruin must stare you in the face. Let us then do what is in our power—*amend and enlarge the confederation, but not alter the federal system.* The people expect this, and no more. We all agree in the necessity of a more efficient government—and cannot this be done? Although my state is small, I know and respect its rights, as much, at least, as those who have the honor to represent any of the larger states.

MR. KING was for preserving the States in a subordinate degree, and as far as they could be necessary for the purposes stated by Mr. Ellsworth. He did not think a full answer had been given to those who apprehended a dangerous encroachment on their jurisdictions. Expedients might be devised as he conceived that would give them all the security the nature of things would admit of. In the establishment of Societies the Constitution was to the Legislature what the laws were to individuals. As the fundamental rights of individuals are secure by express provisions in the State Constitutions; why may not a like security be provided for the Rights of States in the National Constitution. The articles of Union between England and Scotland furnish an example of such a provision in favor of sundry rights of Scotland. When that Union was in agitation, the same language of apprehension which has been heard from the smaller States, was in the mouths of the Scotch patriots. The articles however have not been violated and the Scotch have found an increase of prosperity and happiness. He was aware that this will be called a mere *paper security.* He thought it a sufficient answer to say that if fundamental articles of compact, are no sufficient defence against physical power, neither will there be any safety against it if there be no compact. He could not sit down, without taking some notice of the language of the honorable gentleman from Delaware [Mr. Bedford]. It was not he that had uttered a dictatorial language. This intemperance had marked the honorable gentleman himself. It was not he who with a vehemence unprecedented in that House, had declared himself ready to turn his hopes from our common Country, and court the protection of some foreign hand. This too was the language of the Honorable member himself. He was grieved that such a thought had entered into his heart. He was more grieved that such an expression had dropped from his lips. The gentleman could only excuse it to himself on the score of passion. For himself whatever might be his distress, he would never court relief from a foreign power....

MR. GOUVERNEUR MORRIS thought a Committee adviseable as the Convention had been equally divided. He had a stronger reason also. The mode of appointing the second branch tended he was sure to defeat the object of it. What is this object? to check the precipitation, changeableness, and excesses of the first branch. Every man of observation had seen in the democratic branches of the State Legislatures, precipitation—in Congress changeableness, in every department excesses against personal liberty, private property and personal safety. What qualities are necessary to constitute a check in this case? *Abilities* and *virtue*, are equally necessary in both branches. Something more then is now wanted. 1. The checking branch must have a personal interest in checking the other branch, one interest must be opposed to another interest. Vices as they exist, must be turned against each other. 2. It must have great personal property, it must have the aristocratic spirit; it must love to lord it through pride, pride is indeed the great principle that actuates both the poor and the rich. It is this principle which in the former resists, in the latter abuses authority. 3. It should be independent. In Religion the Creature is apt to forget its Creator. That it is otherwise in political affairs, the late debates here are an unhappy proof. The aristocratic body, should be as independent and as firm as the democratic. If the members of it are to revert to a dependence on the democratic choice, the democratic scale will preponderate. All the guards contrived by America have not restrained the Senatorial branches of the Legislatures from a servile complaisance to the democratic. If the second branch is to be dependent we are better without it. To make it independent, it should be for life. It will then do wrong, it will be said. He believed so: He hoped so. The Rich will strive to establish their dominion and enslave the rest. They always did. They always will. The proper security against them is to form them into a separate interest. The two forces will then control each other. Let the rich mix with the poor and in a Commercial Country, they will establish an oligarchy. Take away commerce, and the democracy will triumph. Thus it has been all the world over. So it will be among us. Reason tells us we are but men: and we are not to expect any particular interference of Heaven in our favor. By thus combining and setting apart, the aristocratic interest, the popular interest will be combined against it. There will be a mutual check and mutual security. 4. An independence for life, involves the necessary permanency. If we change our measures no body will trust us: and how avoid a change of measures, but by avoiding a change of men. Ask any man if he confides in Congress, if he confides in the State of Pennsylvania, if he will lend his money or enter into contract? He will tell you no. He sees no stability. He can repose no confidence. If Great Britain were to explain her refusal to treat with us, the same reasoning would be employed.—He disliked the exclusion of the second branch from holding offices. It is dangerous. It is like the imprudent exclusion of the military officers during the war, from civil appointments. It deprives the Executive of the principal source of influence. If danger be apprehended from the Executive what a left-handed way is this of obviating it? If the son, the brother or the friend can be appointed, the danger may be even increased, as the disqualified father *etc.* can then boast of a disinterestedness which he does not possess. Besides shall the best, the most able, the most virtuous citizens not be permitted to hold offices? Who then are to hold them? He was also against paying the Senators. They will pay themselves if they can. If they can not they will be rich and can do without it. Of such the second branch ought to consist; and none but such can compose it if they are not to be paid.—He contended that the Executive should appoint the Senate and fill up vacancies. This gets rid of the difficulty in the present question. You may begin with any ratio you please; it will come to the same thing. The members being independent and for life, may be taken as well from one place as from another.—It should be considered too how the scheme could be carried through the States. He hoped there was strength of mind enough in this House to look truth in the face. He did not hesitate therefore to say that loaves and fishes must bribe the Demogogues. They must be made to expect higher offices under the general than the State Government. A Senate for life will be a noble bait. Without such captivating prospects, the popular leaders will oppose and defeat the plan. He perceived that the first branch was to be chosen by the people of the States: the second by those chosen by the people. Is not here a Government by the States. A Government by Compact between Virginia in the first and second branch; Massachusetts in the first and second branch *etc.* This is going back to mere treaty. It is no Government at all. It is altogether dependent on the States, and will act over again the part which Congress has acted. A firm Government alone can protect our liberties. He fears the influence of the rich. They will have the same effect here as elsewhere if we do not by such a Government keep them within their proper sphere. We should remember that the people never act from reason alone. The Rich will take advantage of their passions and make these the instruments for oppressing them. The Result of the Contest will be a violent aristocracy, or a more violent despotism. The schemes of the Rich will be favored by the extent of the Country. The people in such distant parts can not communicate and act in concert. They will be the dupes of those who have more knowledge and intercourse. The only security against encroachments will be a select and sagacious body of men, instituted to watch against them on all sides. He meant only to hint these observations, without grounding any motion on them.

to be continue...

www.ingramcontent.com/pod-product-compliance
Lightning Source LLC
Chambersburg PA
CBHW080553220526
45466CB00010B/3137